WORLD CLASS
HAPPINESS

DOMINIC KING

CONTENTS

For Wes

CHAPTER 1

INTRODUCTION

WHAT DOES 'WORLDCLASS HAPPINESS' EVEN MEAN?

I f you're going to be world-class at anything in life it may as well be *happiness*. When you think about it, what's more important?

I decided to write this book when it suddenly occurred to me just how happy I was. I wasn't just a bit happy, I was completely and genuinely happy, to the extent where I began wondering whether I was in fact, the happiest person on the planet.

Why do I believe this?

Well, I don't possess a gold medal from the *Happiness World Championships,* and I don't hold any A grades on the subject. As it happens, I'm not even a qualified psychologist, life coach, or self-help guru, but that doesn't mean anything.

Claiming to be the happiest person from a population of 7.7 billion, may seem slightly ridiculous, but I'll explain exactly why I truly believe it, and how it's possible for you to think the same way too.

It's impossible to measure our own happiness against another person's, so maybe the closest we can get is to ask ourselves the question: *would I rather be me, or someone else?*

If we could click our fingers and automatically swap our lives for someone else's, who would you choose?

When I did this, I initially thought about people I knew personally and after a short while I hadn't thought of anyone I would prefer to be. Believing that I perhaps needed to give it more thought, I sat for about five minutes or so expecting a name to pop into my head at any second. After scrolling through my entire friends' list on Facebook and still with no candidates in mind, I decided to open it up to people I didn't personally know. *Film stars, pop stars, athletes, entrepreneurs, T.V. celebrities, comedians, models, politicians, scientists, royalty* and *lottery winners* – you name it I went through them! But the conclusion was, I wouldn't change places with any of them – *not one!*

So, my claim to be the happiest person alive is entirely genuine. It doesn't necessarily mean that everybody else would swap their lives for mine however, and there's likely to be many people in the world who think the same way as me. Good on those people! Let's be clear—I'm not in a competition with anyone, and the more people there are like this the better.

You may be thinking that only one of us can be the true '*happiest person alive*', but that really isn't the case.

Before you tell me I'm wrong, I'm going to ask you a question:

Who is the world's greatest singer?

Some might say *Mariah Carey*, some might choose *Beyonce*, and others may go for *Ed Sheeran*, but who'd be correct?

There's no right or wrong answer because it's all subjective.

On Mother's Day, we often claim to have *'the best mum in the world'*, and we honestly believe it. The reason we know it's true is that we wouldn't swap her for a different mum, even if we could.

So, if *I* can be the happiest person in the world, then so can *you!* I love my life and there are many reasons why. You may assume that I'm just lucky, but happiness is not about luck, it's a choice.

We all have choices and reading this book would be a good one.

IF I HAD ONE WISH...

A question that everyone gets asked at least once in their lifetime is: *what would you do if you only had one wish?* The most common answers are obviously what you'd expect: *I want to be rich, I want to be famous, I want to be successful.*

It makes no difference whether we have one wish, ten wishes, or one hundred because only one wish is necessary – *to be happy.*

My children asked me this very question recently after they'd watched the film *'Bedazzled'* on TV and hopefully my answer made them think.

If you've seen the film and can remember the plot, feel free to skip the next few paragraphs while I bring the others up to speed and tell the story as briefly as I can.

The main character Elliot Richards has an enormous crush on his extremely attractive colleague Alison Gardner. Elliot is the office geek and is having trouble getting Alison to notice him.

The Devil comes to his rescue by granting him seven wishes, but only in exchange for his soul. Elliot accepts the deal and is given a handy device which enables him to return to his original situation if the wish is not going to plan. Unfortunately, the Devil has plans to mess up each of his wishes by including something bad, which creates some great comedy moments.

To find out immediately whether the Devil is genuine he wishes for a Big Mac and Coke. Elliot feels cheated when she (the Devil is female in this film) simply takes him to McDonald's. Six wishes left.

His second wish is to be rich, powerful, and married to Alison, with which he transforms into a Colombian drugs lord. He is indeed rich, powerful, and married to Alison, but unfortunately, she's having an affair with a rival gang member, whose gang will stop at nothing to kill Elliot. Instantly Elliot returns to his former life.

Not wanting to make the same mistake again, Elliot decides that he should become Alison's ideal man for her to love him. The third wish starts just three weeks into their relationship, where we see a kind, compassionate and overly sensitive Elliot showering

Alison with sickly compliments. But his niceness clearly wears thin, and she's unable to take much more. So, when a '*bad boy*' appears and asks her to go for a beer, she takes off with little hesitation, leaving Elliot sobbing on the beach.

After his previous experience, Elliot decides that what women are really after is a man with a macho image and wishes to become a famous sports star. Wish number 4 takes him on the NBA circuit where we see him almost single-handedly winning an important basketball match. Elliot oozes confidence, and he is obviously attracting a great deal of female attention – not least from a news reporter (Alison) who is extremely keen to give him a private interview. Elliot obliges and takes her into the dressing room where we see him preparing to take a shower. However, the Devil has been up to her old tricks, and when he removes his towel to enter the shower, he is startled by the sight of his manhood, which we're to assume isn't particularly manly. Alison quickly makes her excuses and leaves the dressing room in a hurry.

Elliot believes he could be on to a winner with his fifth wish as a handsome, intelligent and extremely popular writer. It isn't difficult to see why Alison falls for his charms at a sophisticated dinner party where we see everyone eating out of his palm. He seems the perfect man, and Alison seems like the perfect girl, and as they leave the party together it appears that everything is at last working out. As the perfect couple enters Elliot's pad, they are suddenly confronted by a man – Elliot's boyfriend. Disbelieving the situation, Elliot passionately kisses his dream girl, but this only confirms the fact – he really is gay.

Lastly, Elliot wishes to be the President of the United States with the aim of improving the world and to get Alison to take him seriously. Unfortunately, the Devil has picked Abraham Lincoln and to make matters worse he is at the theatre on the night of his assassination.

Now Elliot is really annoyed and *wants out* of the contract, but the Devil refuses and insists that he makes his final wish. Reluctantly he makes the wish, but this time he wishes for Alison to live a happy life, with or without him. the Devil informs him that a selfless wish is the only thing that voids the contract and enables him to keep his soul. She also advises that Heaven and Hell can be found on earth and that it's up to humans to choose for themselves.

Feeling positive, Elliot finally asks Alison out only to learn that she is already dating someone else. He decides that it's time to move on with his life and when he arrives home, he runs into his new neighbour Nicole, who is a spitting image of Alison. However, he soon realises that her personality, interests and fashion sense are far more suited to him, and he offers to help her unpack, from which we are to assume a relationship develops, and they live happily ever after.

Despite the film being a lighthearted fictional comedy, the message it carries illustrates perfectly just what is important in life. Sometimes what we think we want isn't always all it's cracked up to be, and what we already have is often priceless. If Elliot's very first wish was just *to be happy*, it wouldn't have mattered what else the Devil had in store for him because he would have been happy with it regardless. Even with something quite unpleasant, it's possible to either change the situation, or if this isn't possible, steps can be made to cope with it.

Some people are happy living a dangerous life because it makes them feel more alive. There are happy people who enjoy being different, happy people with small willies (so I've heard), and of course, we all know of happy homosexuals who have released a massive burden by *coming out of the closet*. In fact, it's possible to be happy if we're rich or poor, good-looking or ugly, ordinary or extraordinary, fat or thin, a picture of health or even on our death bed. No matter what our situation, I believe that happiness is simply a choice, so if our wish is *to be happy*, there really is no reason it shouldn't come true.

LIFE'S A LOTTERY

Usually when something really good or something really bad happens out of the blue, we often use the phrase *'life's a lottery'*, suggesting that whatever has occurred, has done so completely by chance. Often the phrase is misused because most of the time things happen for a reason.

'Things happen for a reason' is another popular phrase, usually suggesting life is all mapped out for us, and in many cases, it's used to make us feel better about our misfortune. But when I say *things happen for a reason*, I don't mean in some kind of mystical force type way, I mean that things often occur because of an action we have or haven't taken, be it by accident or on purpose.

If I bought a lottery ticket this week, my ticket would have the same chance of winning the jackpot as a ticket bought by Dave in London, Sharon in Manchester, Paul in Birmingham, or Doris in a small village that nobody's heard of. It makes no difference if Dave from London won the Jackpot last week, or if Doris has never even won a tenner – our chances for this week's lottery will be completely equal.

However, if Sharon from Manchester was run over by a bus, or if Paul from Birmingham was struck by lightning, then you can imagine people using the phrase *'life's a lottery'*. But maybe in these cases, it wouldn't all be down to just bad luck. Maybe Sharon should have checked left and right before she crossed the road, and maybe Paul shouldn't have been walking his dog in the middle of a field during a thunderstorm! Yes, a bus could lose control and mount the curb, and lightning may strike when we least expect it, but there are often choices we can make to improve our chances of having *good luck* (Maybe buy two lottery tickets. That's a joke – not serious advice) and choices we can make to help us avoid *bad luck*.

I personally don't believe in luck, although I guess we can be in the right place at the right time or the wrong place at the wrong time. The type of luck I'm talking about is that of a lucky number, a pair of lucky pants that a person always wears for a big game or a lucky charm they may wear around their neck to protect them from harm. In this respect, I believe there's no such thing as luck. You may have a different opinion, and that's fine. I'm open-minded enough to accept that I may be wrong, although evidence strongly proves otherwise.

When the game show 'Deal or No Deal' was on television, almost every contestant would talk about saving the boxes with their lucky numbers on, or numbers relating to birthdays or important dates. They all hoped, and many truly believed that these *lucky numbers* would help win them their fortune. Very occasionally it would pay off, but mostly it wouldn't, which suggested strongly that the scenarios were completely random. The game was partly down to luck, but often good choices would determine its outcome.

One of my oldest friends was once a contestant on the show, and he was no different. He's a very smart guy, but even he was talking about important birthday dates that he wanted to save and spoke about a friend's dream involving a certain box containing £75,000 (again I've heard this type of thing said a lot on the show). However, when my friend took the £75,000 out of the game, he said that he no longer believed in the box, which suggested that had it been in play, he may well have believed the dream. As it turned out, my friend made some clever choices and ended up with £32,500, which was a great result. But just like in almost every show, it ended up being his good choices that made the difference, and very little to do with any lucky numbers. Either way, I was really happy for my friend.

Theories on lucky numbers and lucky charms are proved wrong so often, but the evidence is conveniently swept aside and never mentioned.

On the rare occasions when lucky numbers do come up trumps, it's somehow used as confirmation that the theory was correct as opposed to it being coincidental.

Maybe a certain number does provide good fortune for an individual a lot more than others, but that's how a coincidence works.

For instance, if I was to flip a coin ten times and on the first nine flips it lands on *heads*, it doesn't mean that on the tenth flip it is more likely to be *tails*. On the tenth flip, it is still exactly 50/50 just the same as it was on the first flip. *Heads* ten times in a row is unlikely, but it's definitely possible, and if it *does* happen, it wouldn't automatically mean that *heads* is luckier – it would just be a coincidence.

So, what's all this got to do with being happy? Well, if you stand any chance of being truly happy, cast aside any misconception that happy people are just lucky. As I've tried to point out, luck (in my opinion) is just a myth.

If we try to describe someone we know who appears to be truly happy, we are likely to say, *"They're so lucky!"*

Now I can guarantee that *bad things* have happened to *happy people,* just as they have to me. But it's more often than not how we deal with the bad times that count. Finding the positives in every situation and moving forward is the only way to maintain that true happiness. The only way to cope sometimes is to just accept that bad things happen to everyone and that it's all part of life's journey. What we can almost always guarantee though, is that something good is around the corner, as life is often a roller coaster ride. And yes – more bad things may have happened to you than most others, but that's just how it is. Just like how it's possible to spin ten *heads* in a row, it's possible to have ten bad things happen to you in a row. It doesn't make you unlucky and it certainly doesn't mean that you're cursed. Just remember at some point you're bound to spin a *tail*.

If you're unhappy, it's probably because you haven't yet learnt how to take those positive steps to become happy.

Positive action usually results in positive results or reactions. One of my all-time favourite quotes is, *"The harder I work, the luckier I get."* There seems to be some uncertainty as to who actually coined the phrase. Some think it was the golfing legend Gary Player, some believe he took it from fellow golfer Jerry Barber.

There's some dispute whether the original quote contained the word *'work'* at all, as it may well have been, *"The harder I practise the luckier I get."*

However, it makes no difference who said it, or whether the actual quote contained the word *'work'* or *'practise'*. What matters is the moral behind it, as it fits well into all walks of life and is extremely true.

If we slightly adapt the quote, it can easily become, *"The more positive I am the happier I get".*

So, next time anyone asks you why you're unhappy, don't ever answer, *"It's because I'm just unlucky"* because that's utter rubbish!

If you're unhappy, it's probably because you haven't yet learnt how to take those positive steps to become happy.

Forget bad luck because that suggests that we're not in control. We may not be in control of the world around us but believe me, we're 100% in control of the inner game going on between our ears. If we win that game, it's surprising just how often we can create our own luck.

ME

We all have our strengths and weaknesses, and believe me, I have many weaknesses, but I'd like to think I'm pretty self-aware, and I would definitely regard this as one of my strengths. Self-awareness can really contribute to our happiness in my opinion and I will cover this in a later chapter. So, being the *self-aware* guy that I am, I recognise that a chapter about *me*, written by *me*, telling you why it's so great being *me*, is not going to make *you* a great deal happier – which essentially is the idea of the book in the first place. However, I think it's quite important for you to know whom you're taking this advice from, as some areas we'll be covering will relate closely to events that have happened in my life. Hopefully then when I refer to certain things later in the book, it'll make more sense. I'm not some wannabe autobiographer, so I'll try to keep it as brief as I can, while including everything that I think may be relevant – so here goes.

I made my first appearance into the world on 10th March 1978 and was named Dominic Justin King. My older brother Adam came along four years before me, and we were both brought up by our loving parents Terry and Joan.

We all lived happily in our three bedroomed semi-detached house in a village close to Great Yarmouth on the Norfolk coast in England, in the home that our parents still share today.

I look back on my childhood fondly, as myself and Adam were best mates despite the four-year age gap, in a time when health and safety wasn't such a big issue, and we were free to play out without any real fear of the world around us. If we refused cigarettes, didn't get in a stranger's car, and remembered what the *Green Cross Code* man had taught us about crossing roads, we'd be as safe as houses.

When my brother was six years old, my parents took him along to the local judo club because they felt that Adam was easily pushed around by the bigger boys and wanted to prevent him from getting bullied. I was only two years old at the time and was taken along with my parents. Although I was too young to participate I was surprisingly contented to just sit on the side, and never appeared to get bored with watching. I can't really remember this very well, but little did any of us know, that the simple decision to attend the class with my brother, made possibly the biggest impact on all of our lives. Like many siblings do, I followed my brother onto the mat two years later at the age of four and started on a journey that I'm still on today.

Fast forward thirty-seven years and I still do judo. Not just once or twice a week, but every day. Teaching judo is my job, I met my wife through judo, my three children do judo, and my dad especially is still very much involved with the running of my clubs.

My business is called 'Dominic King Judo & MMA Academy' so as you can tell from the name, I teach MMA as well (MMA stands for Mixed Martial Arts).

I loved judo right from the start and it didn't take long before I started winning local competitions. Around about the age of ten, I began to have ambitions to compete in the Olympic Games and it became my ultimate goal to win the gold medal. I still played out with my brother and with other friends, but free time was becoming less frequent as training and competition took over my life.

I became an area champion many times and worked my way up to become the Junior British Champion, which later led to selection for the Youth Olympic Games. I was seventeen years old and this was the biggest competition I could be selected for at the time. Just like the senior Olympic Games, it was a multi-sport event and that week gave me a taste of what I craved as an adult. In the competition, I exceeded my expectations and ended up with the silver medal, which I'm still very proud of to this day.

The following year I began dating my wife Claire, which wasn't as straight forward as it sounds, as she was still only fourteen years old, and I was eighteen. Yes, I know – I've heard all the jokes, although it must have been right because we're still together twenty-three years later and as I've already mentioned, we have three beautiful children, Ryan who's thirteen, Joshua who's eleven and Lucy nine.

Claire joined the judo club at about ten years old, and although I was older, we would regularly be on the same mat together. Claire would often want to be my partner, which maybe wasn't the best thing for my progression, but certainly helped with her judo. As a result, Claire began to win a lot of competitions also, and increased her training evenings, so I would see her on a more regular basis.

I got to know her family quite well, and her dad, who was a Physical Training Instructor at the local prison, offered to train me off the mat by looking after my weight programs and circuit training.

Because he was helping me with my training, I returned the favour by giving Claire more of my time and helping her with her judo. This meant we were spending more time together and things between us started to develop. We took things very slowly in the early stages because of the age difference.

Luckily her parents were cool with it, which was probably because they knew me quite well, so it all worked out in the end. My in-laws are great (which is a phrase you don't hear every day) and we all often holiday together along with the kids.

With Claire being so young at the beginning of our relationship, it gave me time to concentrate on my judo. While I spent time away at International competitions and training camps, Claire was able to concentrate on gaining GCSEs and later went away to university. Claire studied to become a nurse and is now a staff nurse at our local hospital.

During this period, I became the British Senior Champion and at the beginning of 2002 I trained in

Japan with the British Squad. We were all looking for selection for the 2002 Commonwealth Games in Manchester and the place was really between myself and another guy. During one tournament he managed to beat the Olympic Silver medallist by the maximum score, so he ended up getting selected and I had to make do with the reserve spot. It turned out that my rival won the gold medal at the Commonwealth Games, and as I'd beaten him by the maximum score just six months earlier, I was gutted. What made it worse was that I had previously beaten everyone on the podium, and I had nothing to show for it.

I decided to see this as a positive and used it to help me possibly gain selection for the 2004 Olympic Games. I was not quite at that level in 2000, but I had previously beaten our representative from that particular Olympics, so I knew that I was more than capable of making it if I believed in myself. I definitely had the ability, but unfortunately for me, the lack of self-belief was becoming a bit of an issue.

My judo coach arranged for me to see a sports psychologist on a regular basis, and I felt that things started to improve. I was at a British squad training session in May 2003, and I was without a doubt, doing the best judo of my life. During hard randori (which is the judo equivalent of sparring) I was destroying everyone in my path, and I honestly felt unbeatable. I spoke earlier about bad things just happening, and this was one of those occasions for me. Two larger fighters who were involved in their own battle clattered into the side of my knee at speed and I experienced the most excruciating pain that I'd ever felt (at that time anyway). The cruciate ligament in my knee had been completely ruptured, and it took the best part of a year before I recovered completely. When I say recovered completely, I meant the knee. The confidence took longer to return and the climb back up the competitive ladder was tougher than I anticipated.

During my absence, other faces had started to emerge and by the 2004 Olympics I wasn't realistically in contention. This was obviously a blow for me, so I made plans to compete for a place in the Beijing Olympic Games set to take place in 2008. However, for the rest of 2004 and the beginning of 2005 something just didn't feel right. I felt poorly and lethargic often and I then got a bad bout of food poisoning. It took a while before I felt up to training again, but even once I returned, I never felt as though I was firing on all cylinders. I then started to get diarrhoea symptoms again, but I wasn't overly concerned as I was still managing to keep up the training.

It steadily got worse and I went to the doctor, who told me there was nothing to worry about. It continued over the next few weeks, so I returned to the doctor and expressed my concerns because my dad had previously suffered from a condition called ulcerative colitis, which is a serious bowel condition. He sent me away once again and said he thought it was just irritable bowel syndrome, which is far less serious. I accepted the diagnosis and continued with my training and competing. I started to get blood coming from my back passage when I was going to the toilet (apologies if you're eating) and the visits were becoming more and more frequent.

The World Championships in Egypt were coming up in the October and all my previous rivals had retired. I felt that if I was fit then the place should be mine, but I was far from my old self.

Nobody from our weight category had stood out that year, so it was decided that the top thirteen players in the country would compete against one another for the place. I really wanted that place, but by nine on the morning of the competition I had already filled the toilet bowl with blood four times, and I was not in any shape to compete.

I had a really good go and I scraped through against some decent fighters, but my performance was terrible. I've no idea how I did it, but I made it to the last four where I lost to get into the final.

As it happened, it wouldn't have made any difference had I have won that competition, as at the time of the World Championships, I was laid up in a hospital bed where I spent a total of five weeks. It turned out that I *did* in fact have ulcerative colitis. The day before I was admitted to hospital, I had been to the toilet thirty times. Going thirty times in twenty-four hours basically meant that I spent a whole day more or less stuck on the toilet, and with the lack of sleep on top of everything, I wasn't exactly equipped to tackle the five weeks that followed.

The first two weeks were a roller coaster as they pumped me with drugs in the hope that I would go into remission. The toilet trips would slow down, and I was constantly told that I may be going home soon. However, each time they lowered the dosage on the drugs the toilet trips would dramatically increase again.

After two weeks of feeling like I was on this constant treadmill, they made the decision that I was dreading to hear. They were going to remove my large bowel and replace it with an ileostomy bag, which would sit on the front of my belly as it collected my bodily waste. This would then have to be emptied and changed on a regular basis and I knew exactly what that meant for my judo career.

The specialist nurse came to speak to me about how to deal with the change, and Claire, who was pregnant with Ryan at the time, did all the talking. I couldn't bring myself to say a word because I was trying my hardest to hold my emotions in check, as I knew that if I started talking I would become inconsolable. Claire tried her best to ask all the right questions, but the nurse who seemed to want me to open up, asked what was bothering me the most. Was it that I'd look different, or was I worried that Claire wouldn't accept it? Claire turned to the nurse and said, "I know exactly what it is – it's because his judo career's over." The nurse looked back at me and said. "is that the problem?" I still couldn't speak but I think I half nodded as a couple of tears managed to escape from my eyes, and we all just sat in silence as they slowly rolled down my cheeks.

That moment was one of the toughest of my life and I can appreciate that if you've got no interest in sport or have never spent your whole life working towards a goal, I guess it is difficult to understand how it feels to have that dream snatched away. Mentally it was a low point, but over the weeks and months that followed, I experienced the worst physical pain of my life, making the knee injury appear insignificant.

I had four operations in all over an eighteen-month period, and I experienced several complications that included a blockage, a blood clot that required emergency surgery and the surgeon dropping me! We can all laugh about it now, but at the time I think I used some language that is best left to the imagination. After my first operation, the surgeon came around to say that the procedure had been successful and wanted to mention that my torso was the best he'd ever had the pleasure of cutting into. Unfortunately, he caught his foot on the lever that is pressed when a patient has a cardiac arrest and my bed went from maybe a sixty-degree angle to completely flat in a split second. Not a great feeling when you've got about twenty staples holding your body together.

The recovery from this episode was long and slow, and it was made more difficult as Ryan (our first child) was born a short time after. Having a new-born is exhausting at the best of times, but although I wanted fatherhood to be a job I excelled at, I struggled in the early stages. As a competitor, I used to fight in the 66 kg weight category and my body fat was around 5%. The day I left hospital I weighed 53.5 kg and I honestly looked like a skeleton. I felt weaker than I'd ever felt in my life and I needed to use a cushion to sit on a hard chair, as it was just impossible to get comfortable.

Claire was brilliant and had coped tremendously well over those few months. Not only did she have to contend with more physical work than normal as I was less able to help out, she had the mental stress of seeing me in such a bad way and the small task of carrying our child, delivering him (that's another story for later) and then straight into action with motherhood.

Things improved over time, and in February 2007 the bag was eventually removed from my belly, meaning that I was left with an internal pouch. Other than a scar running the length of my stomach, I don't look any different to anybody else now. The scar for me is not an issue, so apart from a couple of extra toilet trips a day I'm more or less back to normal and it doesn't really hold me back. I even got back to competitive judo to a certain extent.

In 2007, I was part of the Eastern Area team that won the National team event, something that the area had never achieved before.

Happiness is
a decision,
and it's easier
than you
probably think.

_____

I officially retired from competition in 2008 after a couple more local competition wins. My fitness was poor due to lack of quality training and my focus had turned to other things. Joshua was born in 2008 and my business (which I started in 2004) was picking up.

I made a brief comeback in 2010 where I won two more local competitions that I entered just for fun, but at one of these events I was more than a little surprised to see a fighter named Ashley Mckenzie turn up. Three months prior to this competition he had beaten the World Champion (in judo this literally means the best fighter in the world, which is not always the case with many other combat sports) and three months later he beat the Olympic Silver Medallist before he made the Olympic team in 2012. On this particular day we both made the final as expected, but what was very unexpected was that I went on to win the final. I was badly lacking fitness, but I had gained a self-belief which had come a decade too late.

I still feel as though I have that self-belief to this day, but although I don't compete any more, I'm now able to channel it into other areas of my life. I feel confident I'm a good husband, a good father and a good judo coach, and I believe that I have some kids on track to achieve great things within the sport. Most importantly of all, I believe I'm a good role model and that's possibly my biggest achievement.

Maybe I've been fortunate to have two great parents that have shown me how to be a decent human being, maybe the love of a good lady has been the key, or maybe it's all the years of judo that has helped to build my character. I'm sure all these things have contributed to the person I am today, but I honestly believe that the bad times have moulded my character and allowed me to appreciate life a whole lot more. I enjoy everything about my life today. I love my wife and kids more than I could ever describe, my family and friends are all fantastic and I have the best job in the world that doesn't ever seem like work. I have always been an extremely happy person, but life just seems to get better. I know there are other bad things lurking around the corner, but I feel that I can cope with anything and I have this strong belief that things will always come good in the end, as long as I keep my chin up and move forward.

Writing this book is my way of moving forward right now. I've had a book published before titled *'Judo Armbars For MMA'*, which is really only for a niche group. However, this book is for everyone as I really want everyone to feel how I feel and be genuinely happy.

I've achieved one or two things in my life that I'm proud of due to hard work, but I'm not some extraordinary guy you'd have no way of relating to. I'm not rich or famous, and my story certainly doesn't warrant an autobiography all by itself.

Like most people, I've been both lucky and unlucky throughout my life, but from now on it makes no difference either way because I have the tools to cope with anything and I know for certain I'll be living a happy life.

Remember happiness is a decision, and it's easier than you probably think.

CHAPTER 2

HEALTH

COPING WITH ILLNESS OR INJURY

We all know there are ways to help us prevent illness, such as eating healthily and taking regular exercise, and there are ways to avoid serious injury, like maybe steering clear of cliff faces or refraining from driving cars at 200 mph. However, there are times when there's nothing we can do — if we're born with a heart problem for example, or if we happen to grow up in an unsafe country surrounded by war. As I mentioned earlier, sometimes bad things can just happen, and often they are out of our control.

Generally, at some point in our lives we'll all be confronted with illness or injury to some degree, so it's a good idea that when it happens, we're mentally prepared and ready to face the challenges it may bring. The reason I say *mentally prepared,* is that coping with illness or injury is not only about the medicine we require, or which exercises we should do, but about thinking positively and looking on the bright side. To think positively when we're in a bad way physically is not as easy as it sounds, and I know this from experience. However, the alternative is to think negatively about our situation, and this really doesn't help in any shape or form.

Very few people tend to consider the mental approach and often they'll be thinking negatively without even realising it. We usually only think about a cure for a physical condition in terms of what the doctor can prescribe us. A doctor would never simply tell us to *think more positively* or to *look on the bright side*. But it's a fact that feeling stressed, tired or run down can cause illness or injury, so why would it not be true that feeling happy, positive and upbeat, can help to cure an illness or repair an injury?

I'm not suggesting for a second that a cancer sufferer should just pull themselves together and everything will be okay, because unfortunately things aren't that simple. However, many children do appear to make miraculous recoveries from life threatening diseases, and I can't help thinking it has something to do with their mentality, which is often very different from that of an adult. To put it simply, a small child does not often understand the seriousness of their condition, as to them, they're just poorly and are only concerned with when they can get back to playing with their toys or with their friends. Adults are often consumed with worry, not just for themselves, but for their kids, their spouse/partner, their parents, or even just for their finances. I've already mentioned how stress, anxiety and depression can contribute to making you ill, so surely, it's possible to exacerbate the symptoms with this type of negative thinking.

A good example of a positive recovery was when my son Ryan broke his leg doing judo at the age of eight. It happened in March 2014 during a practise session, while fighting a girl from the club. Ryan has done judo since the age of three, so was used to throwing, falling and competing, but on this occasion he fell awkwardly as he attempted to avoid his opponent's attack.

Unfortunately, Ryan broke his femur and was probably the most horrific injury I've witnessed in my thirty-seven years of participating in judo. The femur is the largest bone in the body and this type of injury generally only occurs as the result of a large impact such as a car accident.

As you can imagine, Ryan was in tremendous pain and I was extremely worried about how this would affect him physically and mentally. He spent some time in a wheelchair and then later progressed onto crutches, before learning to walk on it once again, although at every stage he wanted to do more than the doctors would allow. Many people said that he was a brave little boy, but to be honest, I believe that his ability to recover so quickly was less to do with him being brave, and more to do with him being a child. By this I don't mean that because his bones were younger they had a better chance of healing quicker, I actually mean that his child mentality prevented him from recognising the seriousness of his injury, and he focused only on getting back to what he wanted to do, rather than what he couldn't do.

During the summer, he was told by the surgeon who had fixed his leg, to avoid running as it could make it worse and hinder his recovery. However, myself and Claire were continuously reigning him in, as running became the least of our worries. Often, we would find

Ryan climbing, trampolining in the garden, or slide tackling his friends who were playing football.

For children, this is probably general behaviour, whereas most adults would see it as reckless. If a doctor were to tell an adult to rest from physical activities for two months, most of us would leave it three months just to be on the safe side.

Several years ago, a friend of mine broke his femur as a result of a motorbike accident, and he still limps to this day. I guess this was why I estimated at least a year off the judo mat for Ryan, but less than seven months later at the beginning of October 2014, Ryan not only entered a judo competition, but won the gold medal in style. I don't mind admitting that I was more than a little worried about how the day would go, but Ryan seemed totally oblivious to his heroics and I'm certain that his leg never even entered his head.

Maybe Ryan was just fortunate, seeing as he hadn't listened to the surgeon, and he hadn't listened to us – but what he did listen to was his body. Although he was running around playing with his friends way ahead of schedule, there was the odd occasion when he *did* push himself too far and the pain caused him to stop, but what it didn't do was put him off getting straight back into the action as soon as the pain had subsided. We could argue that he wasn't learning from his mistakes, or we could look at this childlike mentality as being extremely positive. Either way, we probably need to accept that this type of mentality helped immensely with Ryan's recovery.

Adults have more knowledge and life experience, but this can mean that we make assumptions about what's right for us. Children generally know very little about their injuries or conditions, so they make decisions based on whether something hurts.

It's almost impossible to I think exactly like a child, because they rarely make a conscious decision to be positive regarding their recovery. Their natural positivity helps to aid the physical symptoms, whereas an adult trying to be positive can have the opposite effect. This may sound like a strange thing to say, but I'll explain why this may be the case.

An adult consciously attempting to be positive will often say things like; "I'm not going to worry about it," "I'm not going to be stuck in this wheelchair," or "I'm not going to let this thing beat me."

Firstly, they are focused on the very thing that is causing the problem and even when they say positive things like the examples I have used above, they will still in fact feel quite negative. If you read through those examples again, you will notice that they all include the word **not**. The brain finds it almost impossible to process negatives, so the word **not** may as well be taken out. This would mean that the examples would instead become, "I'm going to worry about it", "I'm going to be stuck in this wheelchair" and "I'm going to let this thing beat me."

We all understand what the word *not* means, so you may find it difficult to believe this is true. So, to prove my point, we're going to do a quick experiment. What I want you to do is follow my next instruction:

Don't think of a pink elephant.

What did you think about? That's right – the only thing you could think about was a *pink elephant,* even when you tried hard not to, meaning your brain had failed to process the negative word. The negative word in this sentence was the word *don't.*

So, when you decide to think or talk positively in any situation, focus only on what you want and not what you don't want.

Change, "I'm not going to be stuck in this wheel-chair," to "I'm going to be up and walking within two weeks" (or whatever your focus may be).

While recovering from illness or injury, it's useful to set goals, just the same as if you're trying to gain something. In a way you are – you're working towards gaining your health back.

I set goals and time frames for myself after my cruciate ligament injury and managed to return to competition sooner than most people would have after such a serious injury, which just like Ryan, I won.

Looking back, I should maybe have used the time more wisely to work harder on my weaknesses. I'd always neglected certain elements of my training, such as my flexibility, visualisation and even specific tech-nical work that I'd considered far too time consuming to master. This was the perfect time for a change, but instead I kept my body strong by going to the gym, did a lot of video analysis, and because my leg felt comfortable to run on fairly soon after my operation, I was back on the road. It was all good training, but it was all stuff that I was already good at, comfortable with and had practised for years.

Possibly the biggest benefit I got from my forced break, was quality time with those closest to me. Usually, everything was organised around training camps and events, and often I would train while I was away on holiday and there was even a time when I was called home because I'd been selected for an event at the last minute. So, for the first time I was able book a holiday abroad for myself and Claire and for once I was able to fully relax, guilt free. That helped me appreciate rest and recovery, and it gave me the chance to reflect on everything I'd achieved up to that point.

I had a similar experience when I was ill in hospital. The situation was far more stressful, but it helped me put things into perspective in terms of what was important in life.

Remember I said at the beginning of this book that I wasn't a qualified psychologist (which is true). But my issue with my lack of belief as a judo competitor, my injuries and my illnesses, drove me to study and learn about psychology. So strangely, the element which was my weakness in my sporting life has become more of a strength today and helps me in many areas of my life. Building this strong mentality is simply like building a muscle, and if we practise thinking and talking positively on a daily basis, it soon becomes our reality.

MINIMISE STRESS AND PREVENT DEPRESSION

There's no doubt in my mind that stress and especially depression is on the rise, and it's said that suicide rates have tripled amongst young adults since the 1950s. But why?

Today we have so many amazing things that help to make our lives so much easier, and we have unlimited access to resources that weren't even thought of back then, so it seems crazy that so many of us struggle to cope with day to day life. In fact, all I seem to hear these days is about depression. If I'm driving my car they'll be discussing it on the radio, if I switch on a TV program there'll be a phone-in about it, if I go on Facebook a fair number of my friends have depression (when last week everything appeared to be going great), and even the Royals are discussing it. *Royals discussing their feelings!* Who would have predicted that a few years ago?

Don't get me wrong, I understand that stress and depression are real feelings, and they're not just made up to receive attention. I realise that telling someone with depression to, *"get a grip"* or to *"just pull yourself together"* will do absolutely no good at all. I'm also not suggesting for a second that people should suffer in silence, but what I am saying is that maybe the fact we all talk about it so much and the fact it's becoming so normal and acceptable isn't necessarily the best thing, in the same way that society has allowed obesity to become normal too.

This doesn't mean I expect everyone to be happy 100% of the time either, but it just seems we've forgotten that it's okay to be sad, and it's normal to feel stressed sometimes. These are natural human emotions and to experience them doesn't automatically mean we have a mental health issue. Extremely happy people, such as Mother Teresa and The Dalai Lama, have both experienced stress and maybe some anxiety too, but found ways to manage it.

Therefore, I've written '*minimise stress*' rather than '*avoid stress*'. We can't avoid stress, it's impossible. However, it's commonly said that *stress is the biggest killer*, so we need to minimise our stress levels wherever we can.

The key is to recognise when we're becoming stressed and to deal with it as soon as possible. Once upon a time, if we started feeling stressed, down in the dumps, or sad, we'd generally have parents, teachers, or bosses telling us to, "*stop being a baby*" and to "*man up*." I've already acknowledged that telling a depressed person to man up is as useful as speaking to them in a foreign language. However, I don't necessarily believe that's true in the early stages.

Unless you experience a sudden tragedy for example, depression generally increases gradually over time. It's unlikely that we're going to be genuinely happy on Monday and chronically depressed on

Tuesday, but because it's a lot more acceptable today, I feel that some people are content with that label (not everybody just to confirm). A label allows people to be sad without anybody being able to tell them to "man up", and less attempt is made to change their patterns of behaviour. I don't believe this is a conscious thing but attaching this label to a person can lead them to assume that the recovery is out of their control. This is a problem, because if we don't manage it early on, those thinking patterns become habits, and before we know it, depression has taken hold and it is more difficult to deal with.

I realise what I'm saying won't necessarily be popular, but it doesn't necessarily make it wrong either.

I've seen a picture on social media many times, of two brain scans side by side. One is dull and the other is lit up like a Christmas tree. One of the brain scans is from a person with depression and the other isn't. The heading reads: *'Depression is real'*.

It seems to me that people are trying to justify it, as though it's proof that they're not pretending, which is not what I'm getting at. I fully understand that depression is a real condition, but in my non-expert view, I believe it may be possible to alter our own brain scans over a period of time with good, consistent patterns of thought. Some patterns of thought will almost certainly spiral towards depression, while patterns of thought in the opposite direction can develop a bulletproof mindset.

We must ask ourselves why most people on anti-depressants are still depressed, which makes me question whether medication is the answer. From what I understand, there *are* a few people who suffer from a chemical imbalance, and maybe those people would require medication, but I would guess that the majority don't. The latter simply need to be more aware of where their focus is going, and we will look at that in more depth later.

Almost every problem has a solution and depression can be solved by taking responsibility and finding help. Once we decide that we're going to be part of the solution, we can find the determination to acquire the knowledge that I believe is necessary to make that transition from victim to problem solver.

You see, this is the difference. Talking about the problem in order to find a solution is good, but complaining about being depressed, blaming the whole world for our situation and using it as an excuse is where I think the issue lies.

We don't necessarily need to speak to anyone at all these days if we're too frightened or embarrassed to admit that we're struggling and feel awkward opening up about our feelings. There's so much useful information online that can help us deal with mental health issues and it's more than possible to self-help. I would totally recommend it even if you feel fine, because it can lead you to all sorts of inspiring information that can help us all improve.

Mental issues are no different to physical conditions in a lot of ways. A few decades ago, if a person injured their back, they'd be expected to lie flat on a board and do very little else for weeks or even months on end. Not surprisingly, a year later they'd still often be experiencing problems. Inactivity creates more problems than it solves and today if we experience physical problems such as a bad back or a sore knee, we're usually encouraged to have physiotherapy, which can be uncomfortable at first, but with time becomes far easier. Even those who suffer a heart attack will find themselves on a treadmill at the earliest opportunity, in order to help prevent future problems.

Taking action to improve our mental health is something we should all consider, just like we would go to the gym to keep our body healthy.

You may believe that some people are naturally more positive than others and to a certain extent they are, but positivity is mostly a learnt and practised behaviour. If you have generally been around positive and happy people all your life there's a good chance that you will be naturally positive as well, meaning that it comes without any difficulty. If you are dragged up by negative role models, inevitably this would be the most likely path for you to follow as well.

However, happy people can experience difficulties or tremendous bad luck throughout their lives too, occasionally shifting their state of mind, and that of the people around them, decreasing moral which can allow negativity to develop, sending those people on the slippery slope towards depression.

Taking action to improve our mental health is something we should all consider, just like we would go to the gym to keep our body healthy.

On the other hand, those with a bad start in life can sometimes turn things around. This can be triggered by a burning desire for change when their back is completely against the wall, or they find a sudden drive to chase a certain goal when an event or role model alters their state of mind, setting them on to the correct path.

We all have the ability to change our state of mind, although often it's done without us even having to try and it's something we've all experienced regardless of our current situation. Try and think back to a time when you've been feeling stressed, anxious or just having a bit of a rubbish day and out of the blue something happens. Now it could be a joke on the radio, or a funny clip on the TV, a friendly gesture, a cuddle from a friend or a partner, some meaningful music, or even something as stupid like a loud fart. All these things, plus probably thousands of others, can quite simply change your state of mind in an instant.

A few months back I was having a bad day (yes, I do have bad days at times) and everything that could go wrong seemed to be going wrong for whatever reason. It was a day when I needed to get certain things done, and not only was I not getting those things done, but due to the circumstances I appeared to be accumulating many more jobs through no fault of my own, and I was more than a little frustrated. Anyway, on this particular day I needed to go to the shop to get something and on the way out Claire added about three things to my shopping list. I sighed and left, but once I entered the shop my phone rang, and it was Claire asking if I minded getting three more items on top of the ones she'd already given me. Normally this wouldn't have bothered me one bit, but due to my bad day, I snapped at Claire and made it clear that I was more than a little pissed off. I shut down my phone and continued shopping, but as my mind was clouded by my complete irritation, I was unable to remember a couple of items from the list. I decided to just wander around the shop in the hope that I would see the item and it would jog my memory. As I aimlessly wandered around the shop focusing on each shelf, a guy who I'd never met before appeared in my peripheral vision. I was aware that he was staring at me, so I turned to face him. He was smiling from ear to ear as he said with a snigger, *"I know that face!"* Initially I assumed I should know who he was, and I was immediately trying to recall where we'd met before. *"The face..."*, he repeated, *"...it's the male shopping face"*. I knew exactly what he was referring to, but just to confirm he continued, *"...the missus has sent you out to buy some bits and you can't remember what the hell they are!"* His complete accuracy coupled with the fact that he was a complete stranger, had me laughing out loud at the time and chuckling to myself on several occasions throughout the day. More importantly, this stranger had completely altered my state of mind, and as a result, *turned my day around. In fact,* when I got home, I told Claire, and she saw the funny side too, enabling me to smooth things over with Claire without directly apologising for my bad attitude on the phone.

So, a small change in your state of mind can make a big difference to your day. Maybe you have problems greater than just a busy day when a few things go wrong – real problems that are affecting your life and I can appreciate what that feels like. However, generally the rule still applies, and I know this because on my very worst day, the day that I mentioned earlier in the book where I felt my life had been ruined due to my ill health, something did happen to change my state of mind, albeit for a short while.

The mention of a loud fart earlier was recalled by my situation in 2005 when I sat depressed in my hospital bed. It is to this day, the worst day of my life, but I can still remember the old boy in the bed next to me unleashing this almighty fart, which vibrated throughout the whole ward. Despite my situation, I vividly remember laughing uncontrollably to myself, which went some way to snapping me back to reality and setting my mind back onto a more positive road. Yes, I know, I need to grow up a bit, but it worked for me so that was all that really mattered at the time.

These examples are proof that something small like a comment from a stranger, or a fart (not *that small* in this case) can shift your state of mind even on an extremely bad day. I'm sure it wouldn't take long for you to think of similar experiences you've had in your own life that have made a sudden shift to your state of mind, resulting in a happier outcome. But what would have happened in these two cases if the stranger hadn't made the comment in the shop, or the old boy hadn't eaten baked beans for lunch? I have little doubt that either day would've improved a great deal. So, the answer is not to hope that someone comes along to change your day, but to train yourself to be able to shift your state of mind when it's required.

Remember, if you're a human being, stress is unavoidable and at times we will all get annoyed, sad or frustrated, no matter whether we're generally positive, or have even read this book. As I mentioned earlier, stress is okay, it's perfectly normal. What is important though, is to recognise the first sign of stress and to address it as soon as possible. Unfortunately, for some people this is slightly more difficult than it sounds, as often people allow stress to build up over time until it becomes a familiar feeling. In fact, it can become so familiar that they no longer see it as stress, believing instead that it's just how they are – their personality. This build-up of stress can often develop and spiral into a deep depression, making it more difficult to feel happy even for a short time.

However, this state of mind is nothing more than a bad habit and as with all habits, it can be horrendously difficult to break. According to my dictionary, the definition of the word *habit* is as follows: ***Something you do often. A habit is something which is bad for you, but which is difficult to stop doing...a serious drug habit.*** This pretty much explains in a couple of short sentences how depression can take a grip of a person. You get sad – you don't address it – it's then less difficult to become sadder – and the feeling becomes the norm. Often, you may know that the feeling's unhelpful, but it's so familiar that it's eventually accepted and the longer you remain in this state of mind the more impossible it'll appear to escape from.

Usually though, there is a point when those people with depression come to a crossroads – a point when they realise they can no longer continue in their current state of mind. Sometimes unfortunately, this point in a person's life results in them taking their own life, as their belief is that there's no other way out and no light at the end of the tunnel.

As I said earlier, I'm no expert on anything that I'm writing about in this book and especially not on the subject of suicide. It's difficult to appreciate the mental trauma these people suffer, which makes it almost impossible for me to judge what individuals should or shouldn't do in those situations.

What I do know for certain, is that there are many extremely happy people living today who were once on the brink of suicide, and for whatever reason, either stopped themselves at the last minute, or failed in their attempt. I've heard several stories where people have used this absolute lowest point as a springboard towards their best times and to a certain extent, I can relate to that.

Knowing that many people have accomplished their dreams after hitting rock bottom should be encouragement for us all and gives us hope in any situation.

Every mountaineer who scales Mount Everest must take that *first step* as part of their journey to the summit. If you're feeling as though your life is like climbing Everest, then that's great, because when you reach a happier place it'll feel even more of an achievement.

You see this is the thing – the more devastating the lows we've experienced, the more grateful we are for the good times, especially when we've had to work hard for them.

The first step is simply to *decide* to be happy. That may be the toughest step of all, but the second step should be something easy, something so easy that we can do it without thinking – *breathing*.

Now this is going to sound pretty silly, but I stole this simple exercise from Mr. Miyagi, the wise old mentor character from the original *'Karate Kid'* films. In Karate Kid part two, Mr. Miyagi's student, Daniel, is going through a tough time with some personal problems, when Miyagi stops Daniel mid rant and says (in Miyagi's accent) *"When you feel life out of focus, always return to basic of life...breathing!...No breathe, no life!"*

Miyagi starts a deep breathing routine and Daniel follows his example. Shortly afterwards, Miyagi turns to Daniel and says, *"Now how feel?"*, to which Daniel replies, *"Better, more focused."*

'The Karate Kid' may only be a film, but next time you're feeling a little stressed, give it a go. Despite being as simple as it gets, it's actually really effective.

The breathing technique will help to make a difference and change the way you feel immediately. If you empty your mind and concentrate on that alone, you can feel yourself relax and the internal chatter becomes quieter and calmer. If you listen very carefully it's just about possible to hear your heart rate slowing down.

It certainly works, but it's not a state that'll last any length of time, so while you're still very relaxed it's important to remember a time when you were happy – not just a bit happy, but the happiest you've ever been in your life. Close your eyes and really see it, as though you are living the moment once again. Try not to see it as a picture, or even a video. Try to imagine yourself there again in the first person. Make sure you're seeing everything in colour and make the colours as bright as you can. Remember all the sounds so that you can really hear them, take in everything you can and feel the memory.

The next stage is to do the same thing over again (including the breathing), only this time instead of a memory, replace it with a dream. Now when I say a dream, I don't mean like *you're about to marry the handsome prince in a castle*. What I want you to imagine is your perfect world, not a fantasy land, but a real place – your perfect scenario if your life turned out just the way you wanted it to. Once again, see every detail clearly, hear every sound, smell, taste and feel every part of it. It may be that your life up to this point has been truly miserable, and maybe you'd struggled with the happy memory part. The dream scenario, however, that's up to you. Everyone can dream and you can make it as big as you wish because it hasn't happened yet. It's your dream, so make it a good one.

So, let's assume you've just given those exercises a go – how did they make you feel? It's quite likely that the breathing exercise lowered your heart rate and in turn made you feel slightly calmer and more relaxed.

But what about the visualising? How did that make you feel? What did it do to your body?

If you did it properly, I'm guessing you felt not only more relaxed, but more energised too, and I'm guessing that your head was up, your shoulders were back and that you were smiling inside, if not for real. In those moments while you were visualising, I'm willing to bet you didn't feel tired at all and for that period you forgot about any problems or issues that you may have in your life right now.

Assuming I was right, and the visualisation *did* alter your physiology. Return to the way that you looked while doing the exercise, and if there was no change before, do it now anyway. Keep your chin up, pull your shoulders back, stand tall and smile. Now without changing a thing physically, try to become upset or feel depressed.

Impossible right?

Remember, we can use this simple technique at any time, but right now I'd like you to try one more exercise:

Think of three things that you're grateful for right now and write them down.

If you're that person who immediately complains because you haven't got anything to be thankful for, you should be ashamed of yourself! If you're wallowing in self-pity because you drive an old banger, you live in a tiny house in a rough part of town, or the kids are driving you mad with their constant bickering, just switch on the TV and tune into a news channel. It wouldn't take long to realise just how lucky you are, because there are vast numbers of people who would trade their life for yours like a shot. There are people in parts of the world who may never have even seen a car, let alone driven in one. There are countless people without anywhere to live who'd think that your *shithole* was a palace, and there are many people from all walks of life, who crave the chance to become a parent, but it just isn't possible.

So now we've cleared that up, it's time to think of those three things you're grateful for. It's a good idea to start each day with this exercise, regardless of whether we're deeply depressed or even consider ourselves to be happy.

It takes five to ten minutes out of our day and it doesn't necessarily need to be the first five to ten minutes (although the earlier the better). How about when we first wake up? A lot of people press snooze on their alarms a number of times. Or if we get up immediately, what about when we're on the toilet, or waiting for the kettle to boil, or waiting for the toast to pop up. I'm sure we could trade five minutes of social media time to make a huge difference to our lives.

Believe me, it *will* make a difference to your life, even if you don't think so now. What you did when you tried those exercises earlier was change your state of mind, just like the stranger did for me in the shop and the old boy did for me on the hospital ward. Remember what happened on both of those occasions? My bad day was turned into a much better one. The difference between these exercises and our experiences, is that a decision is made to alter our state, rather than relying on an outside influence to do it for us.

So, if you've got the ability to change your state of mind, then you've got the ability to change your day, and ultimately your life.

Now, I'm sure none of us are naïve enough to believe that after a bit of deep breathing and some visualisation, a person would be completely free of depression. What I can guarantee is that we're all a product of what we consistently think and practise, and the longer we practise, the more it becomes who we are.

Knowing *how* to think is one thing, but the *practise* is definitely the key component. For example, most people know exactly how to become, slim, fit and healthy, but how many of us are in fact, slim, fit and healthy. Having knowledge on how to do something is worthless unless we use it and take action.

Your ability to visualise may be at an extremely low level at the moment, especially when it involves seeing yourself in a positive way. If you're very stressed, anxious or depressed right now, I would imagine you'd find it a lot easier to visualise yourself sad about something, messing something up, or failing at a task am I right? That's because without even being aware of it, that's how you see yourself every day – that's believable to you, because you've practised time and time again how to see yourself in a negative way.

So, you *can* visualise and you're probably very good at it, you've just been focusing on the wrong things. In a way, you've been training your mind how to be negative over a long period of time and you're probably an expert. Maybe it's become so natural that you now think it's *you*, it's just how you are, you're just unlucky, or you're not good enough.

You may have done it for so long – possibly your whole life, to the extent where you actually feel comfortable with it. If you try to be positive for any length of time it doesn't feel genuine, as though you're trying to be someone you're not. The truth is, we can choose the person we want to be at any stage in our lives, but to become that person it just takes practise, or reprogramming if you prefer to look at it that way.

Maybe you are not overly impressed with the exercises I gave you, perhaps they didn't make a huge difference, maybe a slight one, but not a massive shift. That's to be expected at this stage so don't worry, it takes time and practise.

You may take all of this on board and gain some enthusiasm to give it a try, but there's a problem you need to watch out for and it's ridiculously common. It's a trap that I've fallen for on several occasions and the majority of people fall into this trap, year in, and year out, until eventually they stop bothering because they already know the outcome. I'm talking about New Year's resolutions.

New Year's resolutions are made on the first day of January, generally accompanied by the feeling of *'new year, new me!'*...sound familiar? It's true that most people break their resolutions before we even reach February, which cements their belief that they're no good, a loser, or someone with no discipline.

Discipline is the problem. Who wants to be disciplined? We associate discipline with bad stuff – *getting boring jobs done, doing our homework, not eating chocolate, not drinking alcohol, a hard workout in the gym, going to bed early, getting up early.* Let's be honest, none of that sounds very fun and it all sounds as though it may take a large amount of discipline. Discipline works in the short term, but in the long term (and in many cases not that long term), we become sick of it and feel that it'll be easier just to revert back to how we were before – more comfortable, more familiar, but unfortunately still not happy. This means we remain trapped within this vicious circle.

So, what's the answer?

Pushing ourselves to do something that takes discipline is hard, not just for the average person, but absolutely anyone. What we need instead is a target, or a goal to work towards. Maybe the dream life that you visualised earlier. If the target is specific enough, it's far easier to complete the task in front of you because it's all building towards the target.

For instance, when I used to compete in judo, I found it really easy to train. I literally trained several times a day, every day, but it never felt like a chore. Now I'm in my forties and retired from competition, I find it tough to train, although I still do enough to remain fitter than the average person as it's part of my job as a coach.

So why was it so easy to train all day, every day, but tough to now get on the mat for some light rolling around now and again? Was it just because I was younger and fitter, or was it the fact that I had a goal – a target? I wanted to be the Olympic Champion and every time I went on the mat, or in the gym, or out on the road for a run, I was chasing something. The difference between then and now, is that now I must push myself to train in order to keep a reasonable level of fitness (a very general goal and not at all specific). While I was competing, I didn't really have to push myself, because the goal *pulled* me along, even if I didn't believe it as much as I should have. What those sessions were doing was keeping my dream alive, so I was able to train without a problem.

So, let's go back again to the list of things that would require discipline that I mentioned earlier and see how we could look at each one in a different way.

1. Getting boring jobs done
Don't look at them as boring jobs. Each task could be seen as a stepping stone in the direction of the ultimate goal. Try to look at each one as momentum for the next task, which creates a feeling of progression.

2. Doing our homework
If we see our homework as an obstacle that's preventing us from doing the things you really enjoy, then it will

feel like a complete chore. Instead, we should make it our goal to beat a friend in a certain test or challenge ourselves to achieve 100%. If your ultimate goal is to become a brain surgeon in the future, you may need to become an A grade student.

3. Not eating chocolate

If you love chocolate and decide not to have it, it's bound to feel tough, as it's known to be very addictive. However, the key is not to focus on what you're missing, but instead what you'll gain from avoiding it. If you've previously consumed a lot of chocolate, cutting it out or even reducing the amount you consume can make a positive difference to your health (especially long term), your weight, your energy levels and even your mood. To keep you on the right track, it's helpful to have a specific weight or look that you wish to achieve, but more importantly than that, you need to know why you want it (we'll look into this a bit more specifically later on). Once you achieve your goal, you need to create a new goal to focus on. If this doesn't happen it's more than likely that you'll allow the old habits to resurface, which is extremely common.

4. Not drinking alcohol

Same as above (just replace the word *chocolate* with *alcohol*).

5. A hard workout in the gym.

Once again, if we only focus on the hard workout on a particular day, it will require discipline to complete it and this type of motivation cannot be sustained. Instead, we need to focus on the specific weight or look that we're after, so we're constantly motivated every time we step into the gym. Sometimes, even a certain look may not be specific enough, so it may be helpful to incorporate an event into the goal. For example, we may enter a marathon or even a low-level fun run that keeps us motivated. If we do it for charity and get as many people as we can to sponsor us, it gives us a sense of responsibility, and we'll not want to let down our friends or the charity. Many women use the goal of looking fabulous on their wedding day to get into the best shape possible and it nearly always works because they know *what* they want and *why* they want it. The only problem is, that once the wedding is over and the goal has been achieved, there is no plan or further goal to maintain the look, which often results in them ballooning to an even greater size than before.

6. Going to bed early
In the past, this is something that I wasn't particularly good at, but I've improved on this over the years. Be disciplined and try it for a week, I promise you'll feel the benefits. Hopefully, it'll encourage you to continue, as you'll realise that a small change in your life, that isn't as difficult as you think, will put you in a better place mentally and more ready than ever to become whoever and whatever you desire. Again, tying it in with a specific goal will help a lot.

7. Getting up early

Well obviously, going to bed early and getting up early tend to go hand in hand. It's more difficult to get up early if we've only had four hours sleep and if we're tired, it's far more difficult to get into the correct state of mind. If we get off to a good start each day, we're far more likely to remain positive and be more productive over the next 24 hours.

These are just some examples of how to put ourselves on the right path, away from depression and towards whatever we want from life.

I've suggested that discipline is a bad thing, but of course, that's not the case. During our journey, there'll definitely be tough times when discipline is required, but as long as we focus on the outcome or the reward, it's not quite so difficult. Remember, discipline weighs ounces but regret weighs tons! My judo coach used to say to me, *"Pain is temporary but winning is forever."* He now has that very same quote on the wall of his strength and conditioning gym.

EXERCISE

Exercise – for some, just the word alone can send shivers down the spine and a large majority of people I would say, tend to see exercise in a negative way. We all know the benefits in terms of our health and well-being, but often exercise is associated with physical discomfort and even horrendous pain, to the extent where people would prefer to die young than go through the trauma of getting physically fit.

Throughout the book, I repeatedly suggest that I'm no expert on the subjects I'm writing about, although with exercise I have to admit that this is quite the opposite. Remember, I used to be a high-level judo player and the only way you can compete at that level is to become an elite athlete. It's a sport that requires enormous stamina, speed, muscular endurance, explosive power, and not forgetting superb balance. I've personally been involved with exercise all my life and at my fittest, my resting heart rate was in the thirties (the average is 60-70 beats per minute).

So, on the one hand, I'm the perfect person to give advice on exercise, but on the other hand maybe not. It's a little bit like Stephen Hawking teaching GCSE science without thinking *what's the big deal?*

I'm not trying to be big-headed, I just recognise that it's a subject I may struggle to relate to with the average person because I've never really experienced a normal level of fitness at any time in my life.

As far as I'm aware, Stephen Hawking's knowledge just continued to grow until the end of his life, unlike my fitness. I'm nowhere near as fit than in my competition days and I'm not getting any younger of course, so I probably understand enough about the negativity associated with exercise and how it becomes worse the longer it's neglected.

Despite no longer having this dream driving me on, there's still a certain standard that I won't allow myself to drop below. That doesn't mean I'll always run a specific distance under a certain time, or that I'll always lift above a particular weight. It's more of an unwritten standard – a level of fitness that needs to be maintained in order to fit in with my identity. We all have an identity, by which I'm not talking about our personal details.

Our identity is our own belief about who we are. Has anybody ever suggested you do something only for you to reply, *"no thanks, it's not really me"*? That's because you don't believe that it fits with your identity.

My identity is that of a former athlete who teaches martial arts for a living, and in this position, I feel it's important to stay in shape and be a role model.

A fighter needs to be mentally and physically fit, so it obviously fits with my identity to look strong and act positively, but generally fighters are also expected to be intimidating. This doesn't fit with my identity, so instead I make myself extremely approachable (for children and adults) as a large part of my identity is to be nice, to be upbeat and above all to be happy.

Our identity
or our standards,
which we believe
makes us
who we are,
are entirely
made up.

———————————

Writing this book fits perfectly with my identity, as does looking a certain way. Now it sounds as though I'm extremely vain, as though I spend most of my time in front of the mirror, but I'm the opposite if anything. I think people who take more photographs of themselves than any other person, are quite cringeworthy if I'm honest (apologies if I've just offended half the people reading this). Having said that, I do look in the mirror at times and wonder whether my abs or biceps are shrinking as a result of my pitiful weekly routine. When this happens, I will up my work rate in order to regain that definition, not to post topless photos all over Facebook, but to satisfy my need to stick with this identity.

Think about your own identity. Now before you dismiss the idea that you even have one, think about how you live your life – your standards. Are you some-one that's always on time, or are you always late? Do you always pay your bills on time, or do you sometimes forget? If your identity is to be an organised person then I can guarantee, you'll always be on time and remember to pay your bills. You may see yourself as an organised person, just as I see myself as a role model, and as a result we won't let our standards slip.

The thing is, our identity or our standards, which we believe makes us who we are, are entirely made up. At some point we just decided that this was how we were going to live our lives, even if it were a subconscious decision. However, once you've made the decision that this is your identity – *that this is who you are,* then the standards that fit with that identity will just be maintained. It may or may not take discipline to maintain these standards, but it *will* happen, simply because you won't allow your identity to be compromised.

Generally, our identity is decided on from a young age, when we have less control over our lives. We may have been heavily influenced by our parents, our teachers and even our friends, and although we have ultimately decided on our own identity, what we choose for ourselves usually happens without us ever giving it any conscious thought.

Also, those people who influenced us to choose a certain identity are very often just as oblivious. For instance, if your parents are high achievers and expect you to follow in their footsteps, they may have scolded you for playing computer games and not doing your homework. It may have been that 99% in a test was never enough for them, so as a result you've associated **work** with **achievement** and **play** with **failure**. Due to this upbringing, your identity could be to remain very serious and feel that fun is not for you.

Your parents may have been successful in business, but due to long working hours they never had time for the gym. They may have worked hard to be financially well off and feel resentment towards the skinny, fit, or good-looking types, who work their way up the financial ladder by using their appearance only. As a result, you may well form an identity as a hard worker who has respect only for those who achieve success by using their brain as opposed to their body. The negativity that may be felt towards the gym and gym goers in general, could possibly prevent you from participating in any form of physical exercise.

Remember these are just examples, but it could be as simple as the teacher mocking you for coming last each week in the school cross-country and your identity as a physical loser has developed. None of us enjoys taking part in activities that we feel we're awful at, especially amongst those who we assume know exactly what they're doing. We may want to work out in order to improve our health and fitness, but we really don't wish to look stupid in the process.

However, it really makes no difference what our story is, what our identity represents, or what beliefs we have conjured up during our lifetime, it remains a fact that exercise is good for every one of us. Whether we're young or old, a former athlete or a forty stone couch potato, it's something that should be part of all our lives.

Now before you suggest you should be exempt due to a slight injury or a broken fingernail, please just take a few minutes to YouTube the Paralympic Games. Many of these extraordinary athletes can run faster, jump higher and lift more weight than most of us ever will, and generally with missing limbs or debilitating conditions. Some were athletes before an accident maybe turned their lives upside down, but there are others who were extremely unremarkable in their former lives. A life-changing injury or condition can sometimes transform an ordinary person into an extraordinary person, proving that physical performance is often guided by our mental attitude. In the past, having asthma may have been a valid excuse for not taking part in strenuous activity, as it was thought it may aggravate the symptoms. Paula Radcliffe, the women's world record holder in the marathon is asthmatic, so if it's monitored correctly it should never stand in anyone's way, especially if the training is increased at a sensible rate.

These days even cancer patients are no longer excluded from exercise. Sitting in bed waiting for The Grim Reaper to pay them a visit is a thing of the past. They are now encouraged to exercise and eat healthily in order to either recover or at least extend their lives.

A fantastic example of this was Jane Tomlinson, who was a terminally ill cancer patient. Jane managed to raise almost two million for charity by taking on physical challenges that normal healthy people wouldn't even dream of undertaking. Prior to her diagnosis, she was very much an ordinary person, with an ordinary job and an ordinary life. But while her body was literally dying, her brain refused to give in, and she took on the life of an athlete, as well as continuing to be a loving wife and mother.

I fully appreciate there are those who don't enjoy participating in sport. Nobody really enjoys doing something they find a chore, especially if it hurts a bit, but it may just be that you haven't yet found the sport or activity for you. There are more ways to keep fit and active than just going to the gym or running after work.

You may actually be very good at a sport, even if you've never considered yourself as a sporty person. Quite difficult to believe if you've rarely taken part in any sport throughout your life, but if you think it's impossible, look up a guy called John McAvoy. I only heard his story for the first time recently, but he is a perfect example of someone who has used sport to completely turn his life around.

John McAvoy didn't have the greatest start in life. He wasn't deprived, and he wasn't abused, but his family had strong connections with the criminal underworld. When his father died, his main role models were men who were all heavily involved in crime. John's uncle, Micky McAvoy, had masterminded the robbery of £26 million from the Brinks-Mat's Heathrow depot back in 1983, so knowing little else it was hardly surprising that John followed the same path and was robbing security vans from the age of sixteen. He'd always been determined and ambitious and his vision in life was to commit the world's biggest robbery and then live the high life. He wanted to become a multi-millionaire by the time he was twenty-one, as other family members had done, but he always believed he was different from the others, and he wouldn't get caught. Inevitably he was wrong and by eighteen he found himself behind bars.

John had no intention of changing his ways and waited the two years for his release to continue from where he'd left off. Soon after, he was arrested and jailed again, but due to his underworld connections he was sent to Belmarsh high security unit, which is more or less a prison within a prison, alongside some of Britain's most dangerous criminals. Determined that the system wouldn't break him, he began circuit training in his cell, which was where he spent most of his time. In school, John had only ever been involved in playing football and was by all accounts pretty rubbish, but as this was the only sport he was ever exposed to, he assumed he wasn't a sporty type, especially as he was slightly chubby. So, when he began training in his cell, he had absolutely no idea about what was classed as good and what wasn't. He would regularly complete a thousand press-ups, a thousand sit ups and a thousand burpees, which he used as an escape just to make it through each day. His plan was once again just to bide his time until he was released, so he could continue his life of crime.

However, this all changed one day when he found out that his best friend had been killed on a robbery in Holland. It was the first time he'd ever lost a loved one. From that moment on he vowed to change his ways. After two years of good behaviour, John was sent to a conventional prison in York, where he hit the gym as often as he could. It was at that point he realised just how physically capable he was, as nobody could come close to him during prison fitness competitions.

Around this time, he discovered the indoor rowing machine and as part of a charity event he literally rowed millions of metres during the months that followed. Again, he was unaware of what was regarded as a good level, but when an officer peered over his shoulder one day, he was astounded at what he saw. John wasn't far off some British and world records, and with his newfound confidence, he made it his goal to take some of those records for himself. He broke the British record for rowing the marathon, then he smashed the world record for distance rowed in twenty-four hours.

With his focus firmly on rowing, he was able to see out his time behind bars in a positive way and the day after his release he found himself at London Rowing Club in Putney. John trained alongside high-level rowers while also making a living as a personal trainer. His social circle changed from villains to sports people, and he began to build a better life. Due to some of the more technical aspects of rowing on the water, it became apparent that he wouldn't race at elite level and the reality was that he'd come into the sport just a little too late. Rowing was out of the equation, but John still really wanted to become a professional sportsman at elite level.

His ambitions led him towards Iron Man compe-titions, where he realised it was possible to become a world-class athlete at a later age. Australian Iron Man, Craig Alexander had become World Champion at thirty-nine, so a sport such as this that requires mental resilience as well as cardiovascular capacity, was made for John. He had suffered mental and physical pain every day in prison, and he'd become a master at suffering this type of torture. The only problem was he couldn't swim, and he hadn't ridden a bike since he was twelve, but with his determination to succeed, these were just minor issues. After only six weeks of training, he completed his first Iron Man in a respectable time of just over eleven hours. John is now on a mission to conquer the world record of seven hours and forty-five minutes and continues to close in on that time. He insists he'll not give up until he's got it. Whether John accomplishes his goal is not really the important thing. What is important is he's now on a different path in life and is a very different person due to his commitment to sport. Perhaps just as important is his sporting success is an inspiration to many people. Despite spending most of his time training, John still finds time to visit schools to inspire children with his story and encourages each one of them to participate in a wide variety of sports.

These examples serve as proof that our attitude to exercise is purely mental. We don't necessarily need to compete in marathons or become professional athletes, but we really don't have an excuse not to do anything. We don't need to be good at a sport or activity to enjoy it. If we're moving and it makes us feel good, then it's enough. Any physical activity that raises the heart rate is a good thing, but it's far easier when we're having fun. Physically working hard can mean discomfort and even pain in some cases, but if we're enjoying the activity, we can often distract ourselves from those symptoms. Whether we regularly work out or not, I'm sure we can all relate to a time when we've been so wrapped up in something physical, possibly a play fight with a mate or a game of football with the kids and all of a sudden we realise that we're completely drenched in sweat. Usually in this situation, the enjoyment masks the hard work, although the result is the same.

If possible we should find a sport or activity that requires a certain amount of concentration, like judo for example, or even something as light-hearted as Zumba. It really doesn't matter what it is, if it's right for you and gives you a lift physically and mentally, it's worth doing.

If you currently do no exercise whatsoever, probably the most difficult step will be the first one. The biggest mistake that people constantly make when it comes to exercise is that they fail to take the plunge. Taking action is made into a much bigger deal than it needs to be and obstacles are often created, by saying things like: "I haven't got enough time", "I'm too old", "I haven't got the money", "I need to lose weight first" and even, "I need to get fit first". How anyone can get fit before starting to exercise I really have no idea but believe me I've heard it. Most people who struggle to get to the start line tend to over-complicate their plans, but that's the whole problem, they *plan* but never actually *do*.

What a lot of people tend to forget is that anything is better than nothing, and for some, even getting up off the sofa is a step in the right direction. Even if you've never been active you've no doubt heard very active people talk about exercise being addictive and it's probably very difficult to believe until you've been in that position. But it really is addictive and even if you're a couch potato today, it's more than possible for you to become one of those addicts in the future. Once you put yourself on that road, each step becomes easier and no matter where you start from you will almost certainly notice results. It's the results that enable us to build momentum, and momentum carries us to the next level. This progression inevitably improves our confidence, and we feel encouraged to take on more exercise that gains further results, giving us more momentum, and the cycle continues.

Making the first step is the key, and enjoying it is what keeps us doing it. However, no matter how enthusiastic you are about an activity, there'll always be that time when you feel less motivated and it would be much easier to stay in and watch the telly. These are the most important days to act, as anyone can work out when they feel like it, but the ones who get the greatest rewards are those who will do it no matter what. Nearly always you'll come away feeling fresher than when you went in, but even when it feels horrendous, mentally you'll feel proud of yourself and the momentum continues.

The reason why most people start out with good intentions (almost every January) and then gradually lose interest (February if they're lucky) is that the novelty wears off, and they fail to set any kind of goal. I did mention this earlier in the book when I suggested thinking about a certain weight or shape that you are looking to achieve, and once you have it, make further goals with which to maintain what you already have. Maybe you could become a role model for your friends, and you could even help them to train in order to gain a similar result.

Too often I hear people talk about the pressure to look a certain way, and they blame magazines and the media and insist that every photo must be photoshopped. I agree there's a certain amount of that going on, but it's also a cop-out to suggest that whatever we do, we will never look as good as we're supposed to. Many people may not like that opinion, but if we want things to change, sometimes we must deal with the reality, even if sometimes we don't like hearing it. Just remember, I'm writing this book because I want to help people, not because I wish to put others down.

As I mentioned earlier, it's much easier to motivate yourself to exercise if it's part of the lifestyle you need to achieve true happiness. Probably the most famous and successful gym goer of all time is Arnold Schwarzenegger. Of course, for him going to the gym was the biggest part of his identity and as his goals required him to spend five to six hours at the gym every day, it was obvious that he would be motivated. He says that he was always motivated, and people would ask why he was always smiling at the gym when all the other guys look sour faced and pissed off. He replied that he loved being there as he knew that every single set, and every single rep, was bringing him a step closer to making his vision a reality.

Another of Arnold's strengths was that he was able to endure tremendous pain throughout his workouts, and he would cleverly associate the pain with progression, so he wanted to feel pain and saw it as a positive thing.

I'm not suggesting we all need to strive to be the next Arnold Schwarzenegger when it comes to exercise, but we all need to find something to motivate us to do something active in the first instance, and then be sure we have a goal to work towards to keep the motivation strong. It may be we want to look a certain way by the pool or on the beach come the summer, or it may be we're determined to win the mum's/dad's race at our child's sports day, or maybe a plan to run our first marathon in our seventies. It could be a massive vision like Arnie's, or it could just be a tiny stepping stone to gain momentum. Use whatever works for you because everyone will be motivated by different things.

The most common excuse for not exercising is a lack of time. We always believe we haven't got the time because we feel as though we only just squeeze everything into our day even when we're not exercising, so we assume there'll be no time possible when we could fit it into our schedule. But the simple answer is *to make time.* You may be thinking "but where? I can't conjure up another hour or two from nowhere!"

Believe me, you can make time if you want to. The reason I know this to be true is that I've done it and

I bet every parent out there can relate to this story. Back in the day, I was trying to juggle my training alongside running my business while making a life with Claire. I felt rushed off my feet and seemed to be chasing my tail from the moment I got up to the moment I went to bed. Then, we had our first child, and within six months I was looking back on my former life wondering what on earth I used to do to be so busy. Back then, I had absolutely no idea what being busy even meant because as a parent, and despite probably having double the workload, I was once again squeezing everything into the twenty-four hours available.

The boot of my car is the same. With every car I've ever owned the boot has increased in size, but no matter how big they get my training equipment is always squeezed inside until there's absolutely no more space.

So, the point I'm making is that even with a thirty-hour day, or a fifty-hour day, those same people would still complain they didn't have the time available to exercise.

I once saw an interview with Arnold Schwarzenegger talking about the same subject. He said that when he was the Governor of California, he still trained at least an hour a day. He also mentioned that the American President worked out (Obama at the time) as did the Pope, and if they could find the time, so could we.

Obviously, this interview was meant to inspire everyone into action, but in the comments attached to the video, a lady wrote, "Yeah but, I bet the President and the Pope get all their washing and meals done for them every day!" This did make me chuckle because it shows that some people will always have an excuse for not taking action.

The correct mindset is what gets us onto that path in the first place and very soon it begins to become part of the routine. Eventually, we don't need to wrestle with the question *should I or shouldn't I?* It will no longer require a decision because if we're consistent over a period of time, exercise becomes a habit.

After I had stopped competing for a while and my training sessions were becoming less regular, a friend of mine who was also a judo coach and ex competitor asked me if I still worked out, as I still looked in pretty good shape. I told him I was unfit due to never getting time to train as much as I'd like to. His reply has stuck with me from that day and the result is that I find more time nowadays. He simply said *"Make it your emergency meeting each day."* In other words, *Make the time!*

Don't think about it – don't plan – *just do it!*

DIET

As a former athlete, this may be a subject you'd expect me to know a lot about. The fact is, I know more about it now than when I was competing, although I'm far from what you'd call *an expert* on the subject.

Most elite sports people are meticulous when it comes to their diet, but if I'm honest, this was an area that

I probably failed to pay enough attention to, although at the time it didn't seem particularly important. Ludicrous when you think about it, as every percentage count at that level. I was taught for many years how to throw a person from every conceivable angle and to physically train my body into peak condition, but in terms of diet, I had very little access to experts who could help educate me on the importance of eating and drinking correctly.

Don't get me wrong, I wasn't brought up on take-aways and junk food and my mum used to cook meals every day, which usually included a variety of vege-tables. However, neither of my parents come from a sporting background so naturally, there was no science involved in what was prepared for us. But despite rarely having sweets as a kid, I would often have unhealthy snacks such as crisps and biscuits between meals and very rarely ate fruit. Occasionally there'd be some in the house, but generally, it was left to rot in the bowl and often it would just be thrown away. It's not that I disliked fruit, it was just that there were snacks that I preferred, and as I was never overweight, I never considered my diet to be a problem.

Unfortunately for me, that was probably part of the problem. I can imagine many of you scoffing at that comment and understandably so. If you're prone to putting on weight, I guess it's difficult to imagine that looking down and seeing your abdominal muscles as being much of a problem. It's true that I did work very hard to look that way, but it's also true that I'm one of those people who naturally carries very little fat, so even when I'm less active, all the correct lumps and bumps are in the right place.

I take after my Grandad who was built very much the same, but the training obviously sculptured my shape even more. The problem with looking good on the outside means that anything changing on the inside goes unnoticed and if problems inside the body are ignored over a certain period, complications can arise. Next time you complain about your *beer belly,* your *bingo wings,* or your *muffin tops,* spare a thought for us poor skinny people who remain oblivious to any health problems that may develop later on (now you all really hate me).

Joking aside though, this is more or less what happened to me with my ulcerative colitis. It's a condition caused very often by stress and poor diet, and as stress wasn't a massive feature in my life at that time, everything points to my questionable diet. My dad also had ulcerative colitis as did other members of his family, suggesting that the condition must be hereditary. In fact, it's not, but it does tend to appear within families. If you're slightly confused by that statement then you're not alone, because when the doctor said the same thing to me, it took me a little while to work out the difference. What it means is there's no genetic link, however similar eating habits may well have been passed down through the generations and adopted by each generation.

We all probably know of a skinny family, an athletic looking family, a slightly tubby family and probably even an obese family. It's no coincidence that within most families everyone generally appears to be the same build, even though some are not blood related.

Luckily, Claire was brought up on good eating habits and educated me to some extent, as well as our own children.

There are many different types of diet available out there. So many in fact, that I could easily list them from A-Z (well almost).

A – Atkins Diet

B – Banana Diet

C – Cardiac Diet

D – Detox Diet

E – Egg Diet

F – F-Plan Diet

G – Gluten-Free Diet

H – Hip and Thigh Diet

I – Italian Diet

J – Japanese Diet

K – Kick Start Diet

L – Low Carb Diet

M – Muscle Growth Diet

N – New York Diet

O – Oatmeal Diet

P – Pregnancy Diet

Q – Quick Weight Loss Diet

R – Raw Food Diet

S – Slim Fast Diet

T – Three Day Diet

U – Ultimate Tea Diet

V – Vegetarian Diet

W – Warrior Diet

X – X-Ray Diet (Okay I made that one up, but it
    sounds as though it could be a diet)

Y – Yoga Body Diet

Z – Zero Belly Diet

There are literally hundreds of diets and I'm sure if you follow any one of them correctly, you'd eventually achieve a decent shape. However, becoming a certain shape is one thing, but having the ability to maintain it over a long period is quite another. This is generally the most difficult element and is often where things start to unravel, usually because this period isn't planned for.

We focus on reaching that goal, but beyond that, often no further goals are made as we assume it'll be easy to continue those good habits. But gradually the bad habits start to return, as does the old body shape, leaving us once again with a sense of failure. Once this has happened many times, or even just a few times, we tend to give up trying as we begin to form the belief that we just lack discipline. I'm sure many people can identify with this, but it isn't only about a lack of discipline, it's more about a lack of focus on specific goals.

My parents fall into this category slightly and the phrase "I'll start Monday" was an ongoing joke in our house when I was growing up. I've seen many stand-up comedians joke about this problem and the reason it always gets a laugh is that so many people can identify with it. The common excuses are *"...well it's Wednesday now I can't start now can I"*, and when Monday arrives the excuse becomes *"...well it's October now, it's nearly Christmas"* – It's funny but so common.

Anyway, a few years ago after probably decades of *start Monday's* my mum made a breakthrough to some extent. Over the years she'd lost weight here and there, but not noticeably. When myself and Claire decided to get married she began to lose a bit of weight to feel more confident about being photographed. I think she'd seen a photo or video of herself which she wasn't happy with and that triggered a dramatic shift in her attitude.

This led to a decision to take part in a five-kilo-metre fun run for *Race For Life*. For someone entering her sixties, and with no previous background in sport, this was quite a big step. My parents bought a decent treadmill and against the odds it got used. My dad went on it from time to time, but my mum would get on there without fail every single day. Her first goal was to be able to run the entire five kilometres without stopping and her second goal was to reach ten stone. The last time she'd been at that weight was maybe in her teens and the determination she felt was completely different from any previous attempts to lose weight. I personally noticed a difference in the way she stood, in the way she moved and in the way she spoke, and on top of that, the symptoms from a back problem she'd suffered from for many years had eased considerably.

My mum successfully completed her fun run without stopping and around the same time she finally reached her target weight of ten stone. My parents had been on numerous diets over the years, so before she started I had little reason to believe this one would produce a different result to any of the previous ones, but once my mum had completed the run and finally reached ten stone, I honestly believed she'd cracked it and would remain at that weight for good.

I think at the time, she felt the same way too and the fact she'd come so far on this occasion, I felt there was no turning back. I asked my mum whether she thought she would keep it up, and she said yes. Her reason was that she wanted to see her grandchildren grow up. Now the biggest problem with this goal is that it's completely **non-specific**. Running a race without walking and hitting a target weight of ten stone are very **specific goals**, which is the reason they were easy to accomplish.

Children grow constantly, and sometimes noticeably within as little as a month if they suddenly have a growth spurt, so she would almost certainly get to see them grow up no matter what. If she was more specific and said she wanted to see them become adults, then that's immediately specifying a greater period of time.

So, with no real incentive to continue the diet (or training), it gradually began to slip, and the old habits slowly began to resurface. My mum is now in her seventies and although I've got to give her a lot of credit for accomplishing what she did back then, she probably feels slightly disappointed that she was unable to maintain it for longer.

She's currently on a Slimming World diet and once again it's going pretty well, but constantly setting new goals will help her to remain on the right track hopefully.

It's important to know that I love my mum more than the world, so this story is by no means an attempt to make her look like a failure. Many people often fail to accomplish any form of success when it comes to dieting, so my reason for telling the story in the first place is to highlight the reasons for her success or failure in various cases.

I'm not particularly knowledgeable in regard to any specific diet, but there's a huge number of books and videos that you could get this information from if that's what you're looking for.

What I think needs to be investigated more is the psychological aspect of dieting, because it seems to be the area that is neglected the most, and probably in most cases never even considered.

When most people decide to go on a diet, it's usually triggered by something specific. It could be (as it was for my mum) they've seen a picture or video of themselves that horrifies them or makes them feel ashamed of the way they look. It could be they have a massive takeaway and they throw up all over the kitchen floor, it could be that someone offers them a seat on some public transport because they assume they're pregnant, or it could simply be that time once again – *The New Year.*

There are many reasons why a person will suddenly find the motivation to start a new diet and it's generally triggered by an emotion which shifts their state of mind, causing them to act. There are a few different emotions that may trigger the shift; disappointment, embarrassment or optimism for example, but it's quite likely these emotions will fade quickly, bringing them back to square one. Therefore, most New Year's resolutions are nearly always broken before we reach February.

If a person was to suffer a heart attack out of the blue, it would be a common reaction for a survivor to immediately go on a diet. The emotion triggering this action would obviously be fear, but even this would be no guarantee that within a few short months the person won't revert to their old eating habits. Even a strong emotion such as fear can fade, and new emotions start to take over. These are generally negative emotions linked to the diet, as diets often mean going without foods people enjoy and having to eat food they dislike. These emotions start to become their focus instead and cause them to conjure up excuses for not continuing the diet.

Dieting is very similar to working out, in the sense that it's easy to stick to when you feel like it. The hard task is to be able to continue when you feel less like it.

How many people decide to go training after watching a 'Rocky' film, compared to those people who have just arrived home after a long day at work during a cold winter.

Dieting can be the same. It's easy when you've almost died due to health complications, but it's not so easy when you're the only one eating *rabbit food* over the Christmas period. Most people find they can remain disciplined for a short period of time, but it's far more difficult to sustain indefinitely, hence why many people fluctuate with their weight.

When it comes to deciding on the correct diet for you, it's important to know what you're setting out to achieve and why you want to achieve it. There's no point following a diet because your mate says it's the best, or your auntie swears by it. Picking a diet is very personal so it's up to you and you shouldn't be influenced by anyone. As I've already said, there are many types of diet you could follow, although some may not be entirely healthy long term, so it's important to do as much research as possible to make sure you pick something suitable and then follow it correctly.

Remember, when goal setting it must be something that pulls you along, rather than something you need to push yourself towards. Motivation will disappear very quickly when you have to push yourself constantly. Being pulled towards something you really want is far easier to maintain, so make the goals specific and as exciting as possible.

Visualising yourself on a beach, looking fantastic in four months' time may be all you need to keep you eating correctly. They say that abs are made in the kitchen and not in the gym. In this situation, you may have a clear picture of yourself turning heads wherever you go. You'd also know exactly when you need to achieve it by, keeping you firmly on track. This could be all it takes for you to continue a diet without cheating, as you can constantly see the reward on the horizon.

If on the other hand you're faced with an extremely bland tasting meal that you are dying to add sugar, salt or mayonnaise to, but you're resisting because you want to be thin, then you're fighting a losing battle from the start. Focusing only on what you're missing out on while chasing a goal that doesn't sound particularly exciting is tough, especially when you have no specific time target.

However, once that goal has been accomplished, there needs to be something put in its place so once again there is a plan for the diet. It may even be you allow yourself some time to relax the diet for a short period, so when you eat a few cheat meals here and there, it isn't against the rules, preventing yourself from feeling guilty. Allowing this into your diet plan can be helpful and you're a lot less likely to stuff yourself silly.

Once you get back on it later (chasing a revised goal), you're no longer starting from scratch, meaning you can reach a desired shape more quickly and it feels less of an effort.

Claire's diet plan is very similar to my current training plan – *there is no real plan.* However, just like me, she has a standard, set only by herself, that she refuses to drop below. Claire has never been fat, let alone overweight, yet she has never in her life been on what you would call a *conventional diet.*

She was a very active girl in her youth and did judo to a fairly high level until her late teens, but since going to university she has rarely been on the mat, visited a gym, or taken part in regular physical activity and on top of this she's had three children, which is many people's reason for letting their physical appearance slip.

Despite this, she continuously receives compliments from her friends, family and even strangers, who find it difficult to believe how well she's managed to stay slim, toned and irritatingly stretch mark free. I've heard people tell her countless times how lucky she is, which to some extent is slightly unfair, as I can vouch for the fact that she isn't *just lucky*. Maybe they have a point with the stretch marks, but this unwritten standard Claire has for herself doesn't represent a particular weight. It's just her belief that people should look a certain way, and if they don't, they are probably doing something incorrectly.

She isn't one for following *beach body diet plans* from celebrity magazines, nor does she frown upon anyone who chooses otherwise. What she does do however, is every so often she'll look in the mirror and if she's not entirely happy with what she's looking at, or if her clothes start to feel a little tight, she feels she needs to do something about it. We do have weighing scales in our house from when we used to compete in judo and when we fought within a certain weight class, but now they usually sit there completely unused.

Our children compete in judo competitions nowadays, but they're far too young to worry about sticking to a certain weight because they need to grow naturally, so to be honest, we don't really need the scales at all.

Weighing scales can be counterproductive when people wish to become healthier, simply because it's often confused that lighter means better. Even with far greater information out there than ever before, people still forget (or don't actually know) that muscle weighs more than fat, meaning you can be in far better shape and look lighter, when in actual fact you may be heavier on the scales.

So, what does action does Claire take?

Well, she doesn't race out to the local gym and sign up for the *unlimited gold standard membership*, nor does she go for daily ten mile runs. She certainly doesn't cut out all carbs, eat leaves or get depressed due to continuous hunger pains.

So, how can she possibly be in such good shape?

Well, it really isn't complicated, in fact, it's very simple.

She moves more, and she eats less!

If you just let out a groan at the simplicity of her amazing strategy, then I'm sorry to disappoint you. Unfortunately, a tablet that you can swallow after your takeaway to prevent calories from being added doesn't exist yet. Sorry about that!

Apologies for the attitude, but occasionally we all need a reality check.

Sometimes the reason a lot of people fail with their diet, and with exercise for that matter, is they make it far too complicated.

When I say that Claire moves more, it's as simple as walking to work rather than driving, taking the stairs instead of the lift, playing with the kids on the trampoline in the garden rather than watching a film, suggesting a family bike ride rather than going to the cinema, and maybe doing five minutes of sit-ups, crunches or leg raises before bedtime. You don't need to be an Olympic athlete for any of that and it's easy to get used to this small increase.

I also said she eats less, which isn't strictly true. What I mean by *less* is *less rubbish*. In fact, she probably eats more because she's more active, but everything is good, healthy food instead of unhealthy snacks. Fortunately, Claire is a great cook and enjoys experimenting in the kitchen, which means that as a family, we tend to eat a lot of fresh food as opposed to processed ready meals. Too often these days, people will settle for highly processed convenience food, mostly due to laziness and a belief that home cooking is far too time-consuming. The modern world seems to be a race against time for most of us and while focusing on a job, money, a dream, a social life, or even just our favourite TV program, our priorities can get confused. None of the above is worth a lot without our health, so maybe that should be given the most time.

I've witnessed Claire prepare healthy meals within minutes, so with the right know-how, time is not always an issue (if you can't cook, then again, the internet is probably the quickest and easiest way to acquire new ideas). I'm not suggesting all home-cooked meals can be whipped up just like that, but Claire has always said to me it's about thinking ahead in terms of what to eat and making time to prepare it.

She has always been fairly organised and very efficient, and as a staff nurse, she has become very skilled at multi-tasking. Growing up, I barely remember preparing anything in the way of food and my cooking skills never went beyond making beans on toast or pouring boiling water into a Pot Noodle. It's safe to say I was no Jamie Oliver, but over the years I've picked up a number of tips and although I still hate cooking to this day, I can, and will when it's necessary.

Claire will continue to be quite strict with herself until she's happy with the way she looks again. She then tends to relax the diet once more, allowing herself a little bit of what she fancies, while continuing with the healthy foods such as fruit and veg.

However, probably the biggest difference between Claire and many people is she never tends to overeat. She usually eats before she gets really hungry, but as soon as she's satisfied, she'll stop. With unhealthy foods such as biscuits, she'll always be able to stop at one or two, or if we have cake, she'll be more than satisfied with a small slice. I have to admit, biscuits are definitely my weakness and in the past, I have been known to eat several in a row. Having said that, I often hear people say they can easily polish off a packet of biscuits during a film, which even I think is overindulgent.

I guess it comes back to the personal standards' thing again. I'm sure there'll be people reading this now who'll believe this is nothing out of the ordinary and that *we* are the strange ones. In fact, these days we are without a doubt in the minority (especially Claire), but being in the minority doesn't always make you wrong. Apparently 63% of adults in England are overweight or obese right now and it's unlikely those statistics will decrease any time soon. America is obviously far worse, and during our holiday to Disney World, we witnessed numerous obese kids shovelling down more food than our entire family each mealtime. In recent times I've tried to be more like Claire, and hitting forty made me far more health-conscious, as I hope to enjoy the second half of my life every bit as much as the first.

A healthy life often means a happy life, so why not eat as though your life depends on it, because as we all know, it usually does. However, this book is all about being happy, so if you can honestly say that being big makes you happy, then who am I to tell you to live any differently. There are some countries where being large is celebrated, so not every fat person is pretending they're happy when in reality they're completely miserable. But remember, don't confuse happiness for pleasure as they're quite different. Eating a whole tub of ice cream can bring you a lot of pleasure, but what often follows is frustration, guilt and even misery. True happiness will last longer than five minutes and is more often than not a result of our good decisions.

REST AND SLEEP

Resting and sleeping are two of the most important things we can do to contribute to our health and well-being. Both should be simple, so it's strange that many of us find them so difficult and often fail to get enough of either.

Personally, I've always been a night person, so I guess my sleeping habits are not necessarily a shining example of how it should be done. Like all kids, I hated going to bed early and I couldn't wait for the day when I could choose my own bedtime. In school holidays I used to love staying up until the early hours with my brother and then laying in until lunchtime. I also remember laying-in on weekends that didn't involve judo (which were few and far between) and I really couldn't understand people who got up at the crack of dawn, especially if they didn't have to.

The thoughts of a lay-in nowadays is still very appealing, but for some reason even on days when it's possible, my mind and body won't allow me to sleep much later than about 9 a.m. and I'm usually up and about way before then.

I'm not the best at getting to bed early and just as many of you may have problems sticking to the gym or have issues maintaining a healthy eating plan, I have to confess that despite on many occasions vowing to get to bed earlier more often, I have consistently reverted to old habits on each occasion.

I know I **should** get to bed on time, and I know that I **could** get to bed on time, and I **would** if it wasn't for......

......does this sound familiar? Who am I to give out advice if I can't practise what I preach?

Okay, I'm not perfect either. I know what's right, and I also know that *should, could and would* count for nothing.

So, from today, I *will* follow any advice that I give on this subject – it's got to be done!

Anyway, that's enough self-talk.

One of my favourite videos on the internet is of Arnold Schwarzenegger's six rules for success. I will talk about this video more later, as it was probably responsible for one of the biggest shifts in my thinking throughout my entire life. Arnold, as I'm sure you're aware is an extremely successful man and even if you don't know the details of his story, there's still a good chance that you know who he is.

Arnie's *rule number five is* **Work your butt off.**

This rule obviously applies to his training, his work as an actor and as a politician. However, he also says we should get no more than six hours sleep a night and if we think we need more than that, then we just need to *sleep faster.* This is his way of saying that if we sleep any more than six hours then we're just wasting valuable time.

Not too many people would argue with Arnie, but just because he's very successful, it doesn't necessarily mean he's correct about this, and although he's an expert on several things, sleep maybe isn't one of them. Six hours may well have been the ideal amount for Arnie, and let's be honest, even if it wasn't, it didn't appear to hold him back.

Most people would probably say they needed more than six hours to be at their best, but some people seem to do just fine with that amount. The former Prime Minister, Margaret Thatcher, functioned perfectly well on as little as four hours a night.

In most cases, a lack of sleep will usually lead to tiredness that is not only felt by the individual but is often detected by others as well.

Extraordinary people like Arnold Schwarzenegger and Margaret Thatcher are generally so driven that they become used to putting tiredness to the back of their minds or it may even go completely unnoticed until it's time to go to sleep. I'm certain there would've been times when they must have felt enormous tiredness, but because their personal mission meant so much to them, the tiredness was never openly apparent.

Occasionally we've seen celebrities and possibly even friends go off the rails and spend night after night at wild parties. This type of behaviour usually has consequences eventually and can sometimes even result in a breakdown. There may be a number of things that contribute to the breakdown, but a lack of sleep is often high on the list. A lack of sleep in a case like this is far more likely to have a negative impact because it's caused by negative action.

Tiredness experienced by Schwarzenegger and Thatcher was the result of positive action, so tiredness in this instance can almost be seen as a good thing.

It's well known that a lack of sleep can lead to a person suffering from high blood pressure, diabetes, obesity and heart disease, not to mention fatigue, anxiety, and depression. However, Margaret Thatcher lived until she was eighty-seven years old and Arnie still appears to be going strong in his seventies.

All this is just my opinion, but the following advice is from the real experts on the subject:

"Sleep is like exercise or eating well: You need to prioritise it and build it into your day. Sleep is vital and one of the most important things you can do for your physical and mental health."

- **Dr. Scott Kutscher**, Assistant Professor of Sleep and Neurology at Vanderbilt University Medical Center

"Consistent schedule. Consistent schedule. Consistent schedule! Set your alarm clock to go to bed."

- **Dr. Russell Sanna**, Harvard Medical School's Division of Sleep Medicine

"Get some exercise any time of the day. Even a 10-15 minute walk each day could help you sleep better."

- **Dr. Russell Rosenberg**, Chair, National Sleep foundation

"Napping can help stave off the exhaustion from not getting enough night-time sleep. It can increase your cognition by promoting the same level of memory improvement as a full night of sleep. It helps to process your emotions, so you not only think better, but you feel better after a nap. I would recommend people nap for 5 to 30 minutes or 60 to 90 minutes as often as possible. That amount of time will refresh you without letting you wake up groggy."

- Dr. Sara Mednick,
author of *Take a Nap*

Like me, you may be thinking "I knew a lot of that already", but are you doing it? That's what counts at the end of the day *so get on it*! I know for a fact that I function better after a good night sleep, so I need to stop writing now because it's getting late...*see you in the morning.*

Good morning everyone! In case you're wondering, I slept like a log last night and feel much better for it.

Sleep is one thing, but *rest* is quite another, so it's time to think about the amount of rest we may or may not get throughout the day.

When we think about rest, generally we'd picture ourselves on the sofa with our feet up. Some of you may not be able to remember the last time you chilled out on the sofa, especially if you're a working mum for example.

If you do allow yourself the luxury of some chill time then *well done,* but for some, it may seem almost impossible. If you think you fall into the latter category, then it's important to give your mind rest at least. No matter how busy we are each day it should be possible to find a small window of time to allow ourselves to switch off and think of as little as possible – or nothing at all would be ideal. If you must think, try to imagine yourself in a happy place, and try hard not to think about what you've got to do, where you've got to be, or who you've got to meet – just completely relax.

If you don't do this already then try it. If it's new to you then it'll probably feel false and you'll no doubt struggle to genuinely relax. It's quite difficult to relax when you know that you must, a bit like trying to sleep on Christmas Eve as a kid. But like anything else, it takes practise.

I do try to do it myself these days, often on the toilet (apologies for that mental picture), where I just allow myself that period to completely zone out. Once upon a time, I used to really struggle to relax other than when I was asleep and often, I'd be watching a DVD while worrying about something else. Judo was my outlet back then and while I was on the mat, I could escape from everything that had been playing on my mind.

At training camps, I found it almost impossible to relax between sessions and would constantly be planning, or eating, or preparing food, or treating an injury, or taping up for the next session. I used to be so envious of the guys who could literally arrive back at the hotel, roll into bed and sleep continuously until the next session, maybe allowing themselves five minutes to gather up their judo suit and possibly clean their teeth if there was time.

I did have to consciously practise relaxing at the beginning, but I find it a lot easier now. It's important to recharge the batteries and certainly helps to reduce the stress we may be feeling at the time.

Lord Alan Sugar the famous business magnate, author, political adviser and star of *'The Apprentice'*, is undoubtedly a very busy man. You don't become a billionaire without putting in long hours, and with so much on his plate you'd assume he has little or no time to rest or spend time with his family. But in one interview he explained how from Monday to Friday he'd be extremely focused on business but come Friday evening the phone would go off and it wouldn't get turned back on until Monday morning when he'd explode back into action. That's a very disciplined way to manage time, but if he didn't stick to this routine, the rest periods would more than likely never happen – not properly anyway.

Claire and I have always had a fantastic relationship, but some of our arguments in the past have been fuelled by my inability to disconnect myself from training, work, and coaching. As I've already mentioned, I always used to find it difficult to switch off and relax and my time management was awful for a long time.

Nowadays I try harder to separate my time better and I think it's so important, not just to spend time with our family, but to really be present in the moment. What I mean by that is we need to resist the temptation to answer emails, reply to messages or get involved on social media. If it's all related to the rest period then that's fair enough, but if it's work-related for example, it can wait.

You may not allow yourself to relax for an entire weekend, but if you're on an hour break, make sure you rest and switch off. Believe me, a decent break is not a waste of time it's time well spent, as we are likely to be twice as efficient once we get back to the grind anyway.

When we take these scheduled rests (and stick to them), it makes for a happier environment. We feel fresher, less stressed and able to function faster and more clearly. The people around us, whether it be our spouse, our children, our friends, our colleagues, or our employees, will be more positive and more likely to help support us once we get back to more serious matters. Without any form of rest, physically or mentally, it's easy to feel as though our day is never-ending, almost like running on a treadmill that never stops.

Ironically the more we keep going, the less we appear to get done. We need to rest, as the result should allow us to work smarter rather than harder. Just remember, I've been on both sides of the fence, so I know that including this routine into your day is vital if you wish to be truly happy.

CHAPTER 3

RELATIONSHIPS

LOVE YOURSELF

During this chapter, I'll be highlighting the importance of having strong relationships in our lives and how they can contribute to our overall happiness.

When we talk about relationships, we generally think about the ones we share with our spouse, our partner, our kids or our parents. We also tend to think about the relationships we have with our siblings, with other family members, with our friends and neighbours, our teachers and our work colleagues.

However, we often forget about the person we share the closest relationship with whether we like it or not – *ourselves.*

A lot of us will talk about the fantastic relationship we have with our husband, or our mother, or our daughter, or our best friend. Usually, the reason we love them so much is that we deeply connect with them, we know all of their secrets, we can finish their sentences, we know how they think. We care about their problems, we desperately want to please them, and we'd do absolutely anything to protect them. But doesn't that pretty much describe the relationship we have with ourselves?

If we can't genuinely love ourselves, I think it makes it extremely tough to fully love someone else. As a general rule, a person with no love for themselves will feel they are unworthy of receiving another person's love. Remember, you're the one who knows you best, so if your story is that you're not good enough to be loved, then you're less likely to give it out in case it gets returned.

I'm sure we've all had encounters with people who've been horrible to us for absolutely no reason at all and it's likely we've come away from the situation thinking *"what was their problem?"*

It's likely we were not the problem at all and the problem they had, was with themselves. Usually, they won't have an answer as to why they say what they say, or do what they do, as it may not be conscious behaviour. However, over time it becomes programmed into them that this horrible person is simply *just them.*

If you're wondering why you struggle with relationships, it's likely the problem is you, or at least the way you think about yourself. Learning to love yourself, which may not happen overnight, could be a complete game-changer going forward in your life.

We sometimes think about people who love themselves in a derogatory way. We may even have said in the past "eugh!...he loves himself!" But when I talk about loving ourselves, I'm not suggesting that we start acting like some player at a stag do. Loving yourself doesn't have to come across in an extroverted or arrogant way, it's about being the person you'd really like to be.

If right now you're not the person you want to be, think about who you *would* like to be and start acting like them instead. Just walking and moving like them can really help. If you start talking like them and dressing like them, you'll be surprised at the way your behaviour changes and your confidence grows. However, before I start sending you completely down the wrong path, I think it's important to be clear that this must be done fairly subtly. Dressing up in exactly the same outfit as your best friend or your boss and coming out with unique phrases that only they would use, may come across slightly weird, to say the least.

Nowadays I genuinely am the person I want to be, not that this means I don't try to improve myself every day, but I never feel the need to act like anybody else. This wasn't always the case though, as I was far less confident when I was younger and in many ways, I've always been fairly shy. I think most of us become slightly more comfortable in our own skin as we grow older because in general, I think we care less about other people's opinion of us, and we feel less need to put on an act.

I've been told several times that the name Dominic King is pretty cool, and I was even asked by one kid recently if I'd made it up – I guess like a stage name. Nowadays I like it too, as it's not so unusual that people can't pronounce it, but it's not boring either like John Smith for example (big apologies if your name's John Smith).

Once when I was fighting somewhere in Europe the competition organisers kept announcing my name over the loudspeaker as *KING DOMINIC*. You can't get much cooler than that, so as far as names go, I'm happy.

As a child, I hated the name. I hated saying it as it always felt like a bit of a mouthful and other kids for whatever reason could never say it properly. Growing up I was often known as *Dommy* and *Donimic*, which then became Donny and then sometimes shortened to *Don*. I just wanted something simple like Mark or Jason or Darren, which were all quite common back then.

You may be wondering why I'm telling you this. Well, basically my name was just one of several things I wasn't particularly confident about growing up and although I'm more than happy with my appearance today, as a kid that wasn't the case.

I always had big ears as a kid, and it was mentioned on many occasions by the other kids. They weren't enormous so that each day was a living hell or anything, but when I look back on old photos, they were definitely prominent to put it kindly. I think over the years my head kind of caught my ears up, so you probably wouldn't look at me now and immediately notice my ears.

Secondly, I hated my brown hair. Early on I was blonde like my older brother Adam (whose name I preferred by the way), but it didn't take long before it became darker. To me, blonde hair was cool and black hair was cool, but brown hair was just boring (big apologies if you have brown hair and even bigger apologies if your name is John Smith and you have brown hair – I'm sure you have a great personality).

We also grew up in a time when the *mullet* was a cool style and like most kids back then, myself and my brother both had them. I had what can only be described as a brown mop of scruffiness, while Adam had this long *Jason Donovan in Neighbours* type style (which was really cool back then – cool enough to pull Kylie anyway). My brother may not have been dating Kylie, but make no mistake, that hairdo certainly did the trick with the girls from the age of about thirteen upwards and I barely remember him being single throughout his teenage years. Quite the opposite to me in fact, who had to make the excuse that I was simply too busy doing judo to have a girlfriend.

Not only did I feel that Adam was the good-looking one growing up, I thought he was the clever one too. Academically he always produced better results than me, so I guess I felt like a slight failure in the early days and I think it did affect my confidence in some ways.

I had to just be content with being the sporty one, which didn't feel great at the time, but it's brought me to this point now, so it contributes to my current belief that everything works out in the end.

Looking back, for a few reasons (possibly some that I wasn't even aware of), I wasn't the most confident person growing up. However, I was always a natural athlete and with very little practise I could just pick most sports up (except for cricket and swimming for some reason). I was always a fast runner, I could jump well, and I was a good footballer, which I seriously considered playing at a higher level at one stage, as I was often one of the best players in the team without ever attending training (as I was always at judo).

This gave me some credibility as a kid and it opened doors to hang out with a slightly cooler gang at school, and my confidence started to grow as I got older. The fact that I was winning lots of medals in a combat sport didn't do my *street cred* any harm either, gradually this shy and insecure kid was able to hide behind this character that was being created.

To help me with that I would often pretend to be heroes from certain films and mimic the way they moved or talked. On the mat, I would try to replicate the style of my favourite fighter, to the extent where I may have looked overconfident. I hear all the time, people say the best thing is to just be yourself and that's great if you believe in yourself, but if you don't it doesn't work. Talking from experience, pretending to be someone else works.

I would tend to have a Jekyll and Hyde character, where I could sometimes feel super confident and other times feel extremely lacking in confidence. That probably explains why my judo results were so inconsistent over the years, how on one weekend I could beat a world-class player and on another I could lose to someone who wasn't much more than a club player.

So, for me, I guess it was *fake it until you make it*, as nowadays I feel far more confident. Today I really love being me and pretending to be someone else is definitely a thing of the past.

Having said that, I do still carry an element of shyness although it's very much under control these days. It's probably not that easy to detect it unless you know me quite well, but to this day I don't enjoy talking on the phone to people I've never met and I'm not a fan of public speaking, despite standing up in front of groups almost on a daily basis.

If you came to my wedding, you may recall one of the speeches being missing – mine. That's because I wanted to enjoy the day and not spend the whole time having that hanging over me.

The difference for me nowadays is the way I see myself. That's really all that matters at the end of the day, because regardless of what anyone else may think, I feel I'm genuine, I feel I'm capable of more, I feel as though I can achieve more and I like to think I can inspire others to love themselves and become whoever they wish to be.

All I've really done is changed the story I've told myself for many years and my life has changed with it. We all have a story that we tell ourselves and maybe other people too. It's a story about where we're at and why. If you're not where you want to be, that story is generally filled with excuses as to why you're stuck in a certain place and why you can't get out of it.

Let me tell you right now, it's complete and utter rubbish, but it stops you being responsible for your failures. The only way to truly love yourself is to stop trying to kid yourself. Telling yourself you're *big-boned* when you're really just *fat*, doesn't help you get where you really want to be.

We all think certain things about ourselves and whatever we think will be true. Have you ever heard the famous quote by Henry Ford?

"Whether you think you can, or you think you can't, either way you're right."

If at the moment you are thinking you can't do something for whatever reason then you're right, because with that attitude nothing will happen.

Whatever you want to be, or whoever you want to be, just think it. Once again it may feel unrealistic at the moment, but it's probably because you've become so good at thinking the opposite, to the extent you can think it without even trying.

Thoughts are not always true, but they are usually habitual so if you've been telling yourself something untrue for a long, long time it becomes the truth.

To start reprogramming, tell yourself what you want to hear, get amongst people who will tell you what you want to hear (if they don't, just don't listen), and start acting in a way that will make your life change. I watch motivational YouTube videos daily, often while cooking, tidying up or getting dressed in the morning. I find it puts me in a better frame of mind every day and those positive thoughts I have are completely genuine.

Once your head is right and your thoughts are channelled correctly, you'll experience what is known as the *Law of Attraction*. You may well have heard of it and may even have an idea on how it works, but I'll try to explain it as simply as possible to hopefully clarify its meaning.

It's believed that by using positive or negative thoughts, we subsequently invite positive or negative experiences into our lives. I've heard many successful

Thoughts are not always true, but they are usually habitual so if you've been telling yourself something untrue for a long, long time it becomes the truth.

people talk about how they visualised being *a someone* even back when they were a complete nobody, resulting in great things happening and a great life being created. It all sounds very mystical and magical, but I've never been one for believing in any kind of supernatural forces, so I believe it's a lot simpler than that.

One thing I've always believed about myself regardless of any confidence issues I may have had, is that I'm a nice person. I've always tried my best to be nice to everyone and in the past, I think I've done many nice things for other people. In turn, I've always been surrounded by people who are very nice to me: my wife, my kids, my parents, my brother, my friends, my in-laws, my coaches and even my competitors. All of those listed have done some amazing things for me and I often wondered why I was so lucky to have so many good and generous people around me. Is that just a coincidence, or is it because people will nearly always want to be nice to a nice person? If I was a horrible person then would I have been treated so well? I very much doubt it to be honest.

That is partly how it works, if we're happy and positive, we notice happy and positive things, whereas if we're unhappy and negative then the opposite is true. If something is on our mind, we'll see it, while everything else fades into the background, even though it's still there. For instance, think of something you've bought in the past that you liked and maybe you wanted it because you didn't know anyone else who had it. As soon as you buy it you suddenly see it everywhere. This has happened to me with cars, with tracksuits, with trainers, with bags and all sorts of things. The fact is, they were there all the time, but I'd never noticed them before. When we're looking for opportunities to progress, as a person or just in life in general, opportunities just tend to appear. Whereas, if we look for negativity, and we lose all hope of becoming anything, then opportunities pass us by without us ever noticing them.

Remember I mentioned as I kid and as a young adult, I didn't see myself as very academic? If someone had told me I'd be writing books as an adult I would have laughed. But just as my personal story has changed, so have my actions and it's strange how everything now seems to just slot into place. Even when things go wrong, which they inevitably do, I remain confident things will work out okay, and they always do.

Loving and being loved is one of the biggest reasons I'm so happy today and if it's something that's lacking in your life then you can change it. Maybe you don't have a special someone to share your life with right now, maybe your parents no longer feature in your life, maybe you don't have many close friends and maybe the only thing you connect with is an animal or even a thing. That must change and the place to start is with yourself. Everyone deserves to be loved and I'm sure no matter what your opinion of yourself is right now, you have a huge amount of love to give too.

FAMILY

There are two types of family, the one that we were born into and the one that most of us create later. In this section, I'm mainly talking about the family that we were born into, primarily the people we started our lives living with, in my case, my mum, my dad and my brother.

My situation was fairly standard, so I appreciate I may well have been dealt a better hand than some of you. I know these days especially there are all sorts of complicated combinations that often makes up a family, however, if you were raised by people who loved you then you should be able to relate to the things I'm talking about in some way. Of course, I understand there are people who enter the world with nobody to love them or really care for them properly, but that is extremely rare and even in those extreme cases many of them go on to find love in various different ways.

Most of us have a mum and a dad, and possibly siblings, but despite saying that we love them on occasions, they usually remain enormously under appreciated. My parents and my brother have done so much for me during my life, yet like everyone else, I'm sure I've never really told them just how much I love and appreciate them.

Sadly, we have so much time for those people we're trying to impress, the people who may come and go that we forget to give our time to those who really matter, the people who were there when nobody else was and will always be around for as long as they live.

Another great video that I've seen, called *'A valuable lesson for a happier life'*, shows a professor explaining to his students how to prioritise the things we have in our lives. It begins with him entering the lecture room with a bag and out of it he pulls a jar. He says to the class that the jar represents life before producing a tray of golf balls and putting them into the jar until he can fit no more in. He looks up at the class and says *"is this jar full?"* The class are in full agreement with a resounding *"yes!"* The professor then takes a cup from his bag containing many small pebbles and pours them into the jar around the golf balls. *"Is it full now?"* he asks. Again, the class seem pretty sure, and collectively they answer *"yes!"* Once again he goes into his bag and pulls out a small pot of sand before emptying it into the jar around the golf balls and the pebbles. *"And how about now?"* asks the professor with a smile on his face. The group seem pretty sure this time that it really is full, and reply with a fairly positive *"yes!"* The professor chuckles and puts two bottles of beer down on the table. The class begin to laugh as he proceeds to pour them both into the jar. Smiling once again, the professor explains that if the jar represents your life, the golf balls represent the important stuff, like your family, your friends, your health and your passions. The pebbles are the other important things, like your car, your job and your home, and the sand is just everything else, it's just the small stuff. He then goes on to explain that if you put the sand in first, there won't be room for the pebbles, or the golf balls just like in life. He looks slightly more serious when he says, *"If you spend all your energy and time on the small stuff, you won't have time for all the really important things that matter to you."* He continues, *"pay attention to the things that are critical to your happiness, take care of the golf balls first, the really important stuff, set your priorities, because everything else is just sand."* At that point one of the students raises his hand and asks *"Professor, what does the beer represent?"* The rest of the class laughs before the professor replies, *"it goes to show that no matter how full your life may seem to be, there's always room for a couple of beers with a friend."*

It's a great video and it powerfully illustrates the importance of prioritising correctly. It's funny because deep down we all know what the important stuff is, but we're all guilty of taking it for granted a lot of the time. Parents are usually top of that list, because generally, they're the ones who give us the most throughout our lives, whereas often they're the ones who receive the least in return. It's awful when you think about it.

I have to say without any shadow of a doubt, my own parents have been amazing, and I couldn't have wished for better. They did a superb job with me and Adam over the years, we were always good in school, and we never went off the rails growing up. They taught us to make good decisions and more importantly they taught us to give one another respect, and as a result, we were not only brothers but best friends as well.

I'm eternally grateful to them for providing us with such a happy childhood and although I think I *did* appreciate them most of the time growing up, it isn't until we become a parent, we realise just how much time and effort they must have put into us. If I'm half as good as my parents were to me, I'll be satisfied.

Another thing that allows us to appreciate our parents more, is when we gradually see them creep into old age. Both my parents are now in their seventies, which I know isn't super old by today's standards and there's a chance they may have another thirty years in them, but at the same time we have to face the fact that neither of them are youngsters anymore and as each year passes, the time we spend together becomes just a little more precious.

Whilst writing this, I'm obviously aware that some of you may have already lost one or both parents and if you're a grandparent or even a great grandparent, that may well have been some time ago. However, I'm sure there's nothing like losing your parents to realise just how much you appreciated them.

Apart from my grandparents, I haven't yet lost any close relatives, so perhaps I'm not in the best position to judge, but it wasn't until I had serious health issues that I realised just how important my health actually was and how completely unimportant any of my previous problems were. So, if your parents are still with us, then appreciate every moment you spend with them because once they're gone it'll be too late to go back.

Most of the time our siblings are appreciated far less than even our parents. I was lucky enough to get on well with my brother and despite a four-year age gap, we spent more time playing together growing up than we ever did with any of our friends. It seemed very strange to me when I heard friends say that they hated their brother or sister and wished that they weren't around.

Claire and her younger brother used to fight like cat and dog, but are extremely close nowadays, so maybe in most cases as it was with them, things improve as both siblings become more mature.

However, I'm still often staggered by the number of times I hear that someone no longer speaks to their sibling (or even their parents for that matter) due to something trivial.

In some ways, a sibling can't ever be replaced, as in my case, myself and my brother can reminisce about times and experiences that are not the same being shared with my parents, my kids, or even Claire. As the older brother, there's probably even stuff he remembers about me that I don't even recall myself, which I think is why we still have this special relationship I'm sure will remain strong for as long as we live.

So, if you're one of those people who have fallen out or lost touch with your parents or siblings, and they're still around, it's time to think seriously about changing it. I'm not going to sit here and demand that you contact them as that's completely your business, but before you dismiss it, try to imagine now, how you would feel if today you were given the news they'd passed away. In extreme cases, your knee-jerk reaction might be to say *"good riddance."* But be honest with yourself, when you lay in bed at night, will there be the smallest hint of guilt, or regret, or sadness. If you think there may be, you owe it to yourself to at least attempt to contact them to see where it leads. It may not work out, but there's a chance it could be the best decision you have ever made.

If you decide to give the relationship another go, you first need to assess the situation and work out how you got to this point in the first place. Was it one blazing row or an accumulation of things over a long period of time? It doesn't matter who started it, because if you think like that, you won't be able to approach them without the bad feeling boiling away inside you. Whatever has happened in the past, you need to let it go for things to progress. Secondly, you need to try to assess the dispute as if you were them and you were on the opposite side of the fence. That way you may be able to see if things need to change at your end before you make your approach. In other words, what did you do to make them not want any further contact? You may feel you did nothing wrong (which may be true), but do they see it like that? Thirdly, what you need to work out is whether *winning* the argument is more important than love between family members and spending precious time together.

Once you make contact you must leave the past firmly in the past, because constantly bringing up the same issues will continuously send you back to square one. With many arguments, family feuds and even wars, the thing that initially starts it is often trivial, and often leads to the situation escalating until it gets out of control and it seems too late to go back. How many times have you been in an argument and when you try to think back to what started it, you can't even remember? You just know that you're not very happy and it's important to win the argument.

In life, you get what you focus on, so instead of concentrating on any negative feelings that you may have for your family, think about the good times you've previously shared with them. That's how you'll make things up and if you've got a genuine intention to move the relationship forward regardless of the past, the response will probably be positive as well. Often with arguments, it's pride that stops us from making the first move to resolve it and again, I'm sure many of us can relate to a time when all we want to do is make up with a person who we're fighting with but are reluctant to back down. When the other party offer their hand in peace, most of us are more than happy to kiss and make up.

They say that *"you can choose your friends, but you can't choose your family"*, but they also say, *"love conquers all"*. So, love your family, it's the only one you've got, and the last thing you want to do is realise just how important they were when it's too late.

FRIENDSHIPS

O ne of our basic human needs is to have connection with other people and it's essential to fulfil this need if we wish to be truly happy. We can do this in several ways, but friendship is obviously one of the nicest ways in which to do it.

None of us enjoy being completely alone, which is demonstrated while we're still tiny. As children, we'd be confident enough to walk up to other children and have no problem asking *"will you be my friend?" If we were less confident,* we'd maybe edge closer to a child we wanted to play with until interaction was inevitable, resulting in shared play. Either way, we're all after some form of connection and even those who find it difficult connecting with other human beings will nearly always love animals instead.

We all have different personalities and obviously some of us will be more sociable and outgoing than others. Personally, I've always felt so much more comfortable while talking one-on-one with someone, even with the likes of Princess Anne who I met a few years back, but that's just me. I've always been slightly less talkative in groups and strangely I even feel a little self-conscious at family occasions such as weddings at times. You may well be the complete opposite to me, but the rules of social engagement remain the same regardless of our personalities.

There are many techniques that can be used to help to build a rapport with someone, which we'll cover later. These techniques are useful to know when meeting a person for the very first time and for dating in the early stages, but if we're looking to maintain a friendship long term, possibly even for life, we need to think about what it takes to be a good friend in general.

So, what does it take to be a good friend?

1. Treat people how we wish to be treated ourselves
For me, rule number one is the main one to remember if nothing else and says everything it needs to say in just one sentence.

2. Be approachable and friendly
This probably isn't the most important rule of friendship, simply because there are many people with prickly personalities who are more than capable of being good friends but being approachable and friendly enables everyone to feel more comfortable around us. When people are at ease in our company, we're far more likely to build strong friendships.

3. Be understanding
Everyone's different, and we all cope with things in very different ways. For instance, if we kept a pet tarantula we thought was cute and cuddly and loved nothing more than holding it and giving it a stroke, we may find it difficult to understand our friend's phobia of spiders. However, they may enjoy mountain climbing, in which

case they may not be able to understand why our knees start to quiver when we climb a step ladder. Not only will our fears be different from other people's, but also our beliefs, our standards, our tastes, our tolerance of pain etc. So, if a friend is struggling in a certain area of their life, the best way to help is to be understanding. Their problem may seem minuscule to us and perhaps very simple to rectify, but to them, it may be a much bigger deal. Expressing empathy towards a person and allowing them to open up to us may really help them to unload part of the burden, as *"a problem shared is a problem halved"* as they say. The empathy must be genuine though, so it's useful to remember that some of our own problems may seem silly to them also. Dismissing, or even laughing at a friend's problems is not going to make us very popular and just telling someone to *"man up"* rarely has the desired effect.

4. Give advice, not orders

Why is it that other people's problems are so easy to sort out, whereas our own are always more challenging? Most of us seem to know what our politicians should do, and many of us seem to know what the England football manager should do, so it's only natural that we'd know what our friends should do to solve their problems too. The truth is most of us have opinions on all sorts of stuff —sometimes we may be right, sometimes we may be wrong, and sometimes quite frankly, we just haven't got a clue what we're on about. A lot of the time if a friend has a problem we'll genuinely want to help them out, but telling them what they should or shouldn't do, or what they definitely need to do, even if it's correct, can often be incredibly annoying for them, as it suggests we consider ourselves wiser than they are. So often it's probably more likely to help if we just give suggestions instead and ask their opinions on them. That way, it helps them to feel a part of the problem-solving team. I use this strategy with some of my martial arts students. Telling someone to change, or to do something a different way usually suggests they're currently doing it wrong, which nobody likes to hear. However, if I maybe suggest certain ideas, they can often come up with the correct answers themselves. I stole this idea from Angelo Dundee, the boxing trainer of the great Muhammad Ali. Dundee knew that a personality such as Ali would not take kindly to being told what to do when it came to boxing, so if he noticed Ali needed to rotate his hip more while throwing a certain punch for example, he'd say something like "I love the way you're using your hip with that shot", which would inevitably result in Ali throwing the punch using his hip more. By all accounts, Angelo and Muhammad never had a crossed word while working together and remained good friends for life. To a certain extent I'm using the same strategy for writing this book, by constantly pointing out that I'm not an expert on a particular subject, but at the same time suggesting ideas that either work well for me or for others who are successful in that particular field. This means that ultimately, *you're* making the decisions for yourself and you're not being told to do something because I believe I know better.

5. It's not all about us

Sometimes it's difficult to see the world outside the bubble of our own lives. It's very easy to get caught up with what's going on with ourselves and to forget the world doesn't just revolve around us. I've been guilty of this at times as I think most of us have, but it's important to have the self-awareness to recognise early on we may be talking about ourselves slightly too much, or running on too long about a recent holiday, or repeatedly going over our future plans. If we're talking to a close friend, then chances are they'll be genuinely interested, but when it's constantly rammed down their throat it can become irritating, even for the best of friends. If I ever catch myself doing this slightly too much, I'll immediately ask my friend a question about their day or life in general. Getting the balance right means they'll be far more inclined to want to hear about our lives as well, giving us both an opportunity to feel special in the relationship. It's a bit like the "during the war" situation, which is a joke that was used so brilliantly in the sitcom *'Only Fools and Horses'*. As soon as the character, Uncle Albert, starts talking about the war, everybody else immediately makes excuses as to why they've got to be somewhere else as opposed to listening to the story. Our family always found this hilarious, because when I was grow-ing up my grandad was always telling tales about the war, which more often than not fell on deaf ears just like with Uncle Albert. Now as an adult, I understand the significance of what those brave people accomplished during that time and looking back I wish I'd paid more attention. However, the constant reference to that period was probably the reason why we'd all switch off. It was probably a scenario that played out within families everywhere, hence making the joke conjured up by the writers of *'Only Fools and Horses'* such a successful one.

6. Try to be modest

I believe modesty is one of the most likeable qualities a person can have. There's only one thing worse than someone who talks about themselves all the time and that's the person who continuously tells us how great they are as well. Some of the most likeable people I know personally are extremely modest, yet at the same time those people are also very bright, very confident and very successful. We mustn't confuse *modesty* with *putting ourselves down* because the two are completely different. If someone plays themselves down by being modest and later on, we find out they're far better than they originally let on, it makes for a pleasant surprise and endears them to us far more. On the other hand, if someone tells us how great they are, and they turn out to be a disappointment, our opinion of that person generally drops. I would always try to be quite modest on the judo mat and if anyone ever asked if I was any good, I'd say "I'm okay". Letting the judo do the talking made me a lot more friends than enemies and I always got on well with all my biggest rivals, which is quite unusual in a combat sport. However, there are a small percentage of people, such as the fore mentioned Muhammad Ali, Arnold Schwarzenegger and the UFC fighter Conor McGregor, who somehow remain popular, and even likeable, while acting anything but modest. Very few people can pull this off, but these guys can entertain people whether you agree with them or not, and often their boasts are so extreme in many cases you can't help laughing.

7. Don't complain

We all have good days, and we all have bad days and having a moan can in fact, make us feel slightly better at times. But when we complain on a regular basis it can start to become a bad habit until we're almost unaware that we're doing it at all. Once again though, there are those few people who can get away with it. Comedians complain all the time as part of their act, so it seems that humour is often the key to breaking rules. Karl Pilkington from 'An Idiot Abroad' became famous with his constant complaining which led to his own series 'The Moaning of Life'. We covered the importance of being understanding earlier, which is good, but this can wear thin if our friend does nothing other than complain. If it's annoying for us, then you can be sure it would be annoying for our friends too, we need to try to recognise if we're doing it slightly too much. The tell-tale sign is they stop reacting when you tell them you've got a sore throat, or you've got to go out in the rain later, or your bill for the car repair was bloody extortionate.

8. Be trustworthy

This I would say, is one of the most important qualities we need in order to be a good friend. I've known people in the past who are likeable and funny, but quite frankly, I wouldn't have trusted them as far as I could throw them. The way to win someone's trust is to always be honest with them and to follow through on our promises. Friends often tell us things in confidence, and we must respect that. Once they know we'll keep information to ourselves they'll be far more likely to confide in us later. Gossiping within a circle of friends is extremely common, and we all do it to a certain extent. I try to avoid gossip, but if we're within a group it's occasionally impossible not to get drawn into it. On these occasions when possible, I'll try my best to defend the person who isn't present, which is usually who the gossip is about, or I'll at least try to see it from their point of view. That way it sends a message to my friends who are present that I wouldn't stab them in the back if they were the subject of the gossip at a later date. If we have a friend who talks about all our other friends, it does leave us wondering what they may say about us when we're not present.

Another thing I think is important, is paying back money that's owed. I very rarely have borrowed money from friends but on the occasions when I've needed to, I've always made a point of paying them back quickly or as soon as possible. I hate being in debt to people and I'd much rather lend money out than borrow it. Occasionally, I've lent money to people I know I can trust, and I've told them I'm not in a rush to get it back. It's always nice when those people return it a while later, once I've forgotten about it myself.

I think returning possessions is just as important too. We all lend our stuff out from time to time and if things don't come back it can be slightly irritating. Again, if someone lends me something, even something small such as a book, for example, I always try to keep it for as little time as possible and make sure it gets returned in its original condition.

9. Be loyal

The best friends are those we guarantee will be there for us no matter what. Being loyal to a friend is just as important as being loyal in marriage. We won't always agree with our friends' choices and decisions, so just like in marriage we've got to be prepared to take the rough with the smooth. If we're around when they're going through tough times, when others have possibly abandoned them, it shows them we're not just a fair-weather friend. They may not appreciate us at the time, but usually, when it comes to the crunch people know who their true friends are.

10. Don't take friends for granted

I think it's fair to say we all take our friends and family for granted to some extent and strangely it's more likely to happen with those closest to us. Often the more comfortable we are with someone, the less effort we feel we have to make, but what we need to remind ourselves is, how would we feel if the positions were reversed, and we were the ones being taken for granted? If a friend has been particularly helpful or supportive, it may be nice to send them a card or box of chocolates to show our appreciation. Even just a simple thank you can go a long way, and we should be ready to do the same in return when they need us.

You may have read those rules and thought "I know all that, it's all just common sense", but as a wise man once said "common sense isn't actually very common". You may think you already *know* what it takes to be a good friend, but are you actually *doing* what it takes to be a good friend?

DATING

If we know what it takes to be a good friend, we're likely to have more success when it comes to dating. Sometimes (as it was in my situation), a relationship can develop from friendship, which can make the process of dating slightly easier and less awkward.

No matter what the situation, a date can feel as though we're on trial to a certain extent and there's a lot more pressure to show our best qualities. Friends will usually overlook a bad day when we're grumpy or even bad-tempered, but a date would definitely mark it as a *red flag* (a reason not to see us again).

Trying hard to impress a date can often be our downfall, as we can appear nervous and unnatural. Ask yourself the question, why is it always the people we don't fancy who fancy us the most, while the ones we're chasing very often don't want to know? It may be a coincidence, but often it's because we're far more natural and relaxed around those we're less interested in, whereas we become an awkward, bumbling idiot around those we desire.

Meeting someone for the first time or going on a first date is crucial because we only get that one chance to make a first impression and if we mess up it may be the last. No matter whether we're talking about friendship or dating, just being friendly initially is the best way to start building rapport with someone.

You may feel you're a good person and even a nice person, but are you friendly? Being friendly makes you far more approachable and it helps others feel more comfortable around you. If you understand how rapport works, it'll be far easier to make friends initially and possibly seal a second date.

So, what advice can a guy who's been with the same person for well over twenty years and had next to no experience of the dating game previous to that, possibly be able to offer you?

Rapport is the key.

I'd agree that the occasional *date night* with my wife doesn't make me an expert on the subject of dating and is not really relevant anyway, but as a martial arts coach, I practise building and maintaining a rapport with people every single day.

When a child attends one of my classes for the first time, it's my job to instantly become engaged with them and begin building a rapport. Being good at martial arts and knowing how to produce a good fighter is only part of the job. You can be as good as you want, but if you can't get people to return for their second lesson something is seriously wrong and quite possibly it's that failure to connect on the first meeting. Obviously, I'm talking about children at the moment, but building a rapport with the parents is every bit as important, as they will probably be the ones bringing them back and despite what the child thinks, they will ultimately have a lot of influence over the decision to return.

I also teach adults in both judo and MMA and dealing with them is no different. Most of the time we feel comfortable in a situation when the fear element is taken away. With children, fear is often extremely apparent, whereas adults tend to be far better at hiding it. I've spoken to several of my adult members about their first lesson with me and I'm often surprised when some of the more outwardly confident MMA members admit they were in fact petrified.

Overall, I feel I've got a very successful record when it comes to people returning for a second lesson, which probably suggests I'm doing my job properly.

Having a warmth about our personality is actually very little to do with the words we say to someone, but a lot more about the body language we send out. We all use body language whether we realise it or not and surprisingly it makes up 93% of our overall communication, leaving only 7% to represent the words we actually say. So, it doesn't really matter that I'm no Muhammad Ali when it comes to the chit chat, as there are many ways to build a rapport with someone.

How do we build a rapport with someone?

1. Make them feel at ease and you'll feel at ease too
Participating in MMA and dating are both scary in very different ways, but both can be enjoyed once the fear element is under control. When I coach judo or MMA to someone new, I try to focus on making them feel at ease and hopefully provide a good experience for them, rather than simply trying to impress them with *my moves.* Helping your date relax and feel comfortable in your company should be your number one focus. Concentrating on how someone else is feeling, helps you to forget how nervous you feel. It may be possible that you're so nervous it's almost impossible to cover up, so admitting that you're nervous is not necessarily a bad thing. Often, it can work in your favour because if your date is feeling the same way, it's an instant form of rapport. Admitting your nervousness can also work in your favour if you stumble over your words or knock over a drink for example. Your date is far more likely to make allowances and you can almost laugh at yourself, blaming it on the nerves. If someone is nervous when you meet them for the first time, it suggests they care about what you think, which can often be endearing as opposed to awkward.

Body language
doesn't just
influence other
people, it can
also influence
how we feel
ourselves.

_____

2. Smile

The most obvious way to make that first connection, which I'm sure we all know anyway, is to smile. It's one thing knowing it, but it's another thing to do it, and it amazes me how many people will meet others for the first time without any effort to raise a smile. It takes almost no effort and gets the interaction off to a good start. You may say that if you smile it's just fake and some people love this image of being real and frown upon those who appear fake. I understand that, but if you're a friendly person it isn't fake, and if at the moment it feels fake to you, it's because you haven't got into the habit of being friendly. An action becomes habit by repetition, so if it must start off fake in order to become real later on then so be it.

Body language doesn't just influence other people, it can also influence how we feel ourselves. For instance, I've turned up to teach some kids and something has just really annoyed me. When the kids start turning up, I can't let my feelings control my actions, so I may have to *act* friendly and approachable, even if it's the last thing I feel like doing. However, through my performance, my body language convinces me I *am* in fact feeling chilled and happy and within a short space of time, that feeling becomes real again anyway.

A real smile is much more welcoming than a fake one. If you can make your smile a genuine one, it's more likely to have the desired effect. It's very easy to spot the difference if you know what you're looking for, but I think most people instinctively know if a smile is genuine anyway. When someone smiles, we'll obviously see each side of the mouth raise upwards, but this doesn't necessarily mean that the person is joyful or happy. The main tell-tale sign for a fake smile is the lack of eye movement. With a real smile, we'll always see crinkles appear just to the outside of the eyes, as it involves more facial muscles. You'll often see fake smiles when you look at people being photographed, although it can still sometimes be difficult to tell unless you have two photographs (one real and one fake) of the same person.

3. Eye contact

Eye contact is important in those first moments too, as it makes the person feel important and the focus of our attention, plus we appear more confident and friendly at the same time. On the other hand, it's not a good idea to lock eyes with such intensity that the person feels uncomfortable. Not breaking eye contact at all is very unnatural, and we'd be unlikely to get the result we're after.

Eye contact is important while interacting within a group as well (as you may be on a double date or with your date as part of a group). In groups, we must be aware of whom we're looking at and for how long. We may be talking to one person within the group slightly more than the rest, but we still need to make sure we glance equally in everyone's direction as appears natural. Leaving a group member out of a conversation simply by not looking in their direction can alienate that individual, if not the rest of the group. Talking to and making eye contact with only one member of the group is likely to not only alienate the rest of the group, but also the person being singled out. Most people in this situation are more likely to feel awkward than feel special (although maybe not in all cases mind you).

4. Mirroring

If we wish to build rapport with anyone, whether it be a potential friend, a date, someone we're going to teach or even interact with at a business meeting, it's important to remember several things. A person will always respond to us better if we think about mirroring them as much as possible (again without appearing unnatural). This type of technique has been taught by experts all over the world for many years, but it's still surprising how many people have never heard of it.

Mirroring, in case you don't know, is basically the art of copying someone in order to gain a better response. Now I called it an art, because the last thing you want to do is be so obvious they think you're a complete idiot. It's understanding how to do it without the other person even picking up on it, but as a result they are drawn to you without knowing why.

This sort of interaction can be practised just like any other skill, but we all do it anyway to some degree, as it's something we do naturally at times. There's a great deal of nonverbal interaction that goes on between two people who share a great rapport. If you don't know what I mean just watch the way people interact with one another and you'll generally be able to notice if they're in rapport or not. It's usually easy to tell a new couple are in rapport, not just because of any physical touching, but if they're eating in a restaurant, for example, there are often several less obvious tell-tale signs to watch out for.

I've already mentioned smiling and eye contact, but the couple may also be mirroring one another's postures, they may lean in the same direction, they may flick their hair back or scratch their faces around the same time, their facial expressions and gestures may be similar and even their voices may be in sync. I don't mean they speak at the same time, but possibly in the same tone, a similar speed and volume, and they may even use the same terminology. I'm sure many of us can relate to this, how we gradually pick up words and phrases used by our friends and family members. It's common for people to even pick up accents from others they have a rapport with. Claire's family are from the Midlands, and she often slips into the accent while talking to her grandparents and cousins, which can be quite comical at times.

Likewise, though, it sticks out a mile when a couple aren't in rapport, as everything about them is opposite. They tend to face in opposite directions with their feet pointing away from the other person, they walk and talk at different speeds, they interact far less (including touching and eye contact), and these days especially, both parties may seem more occupied by their phones than one another.

Because much of this interaction (or lack of it) happens naturally, it's possible with a little bit of thought to influence other people's unconscious minds by getting them into a rapport with us. In general, we tend to like people who are either *like us* or *like the way we want to be ourselves.* We can confirm this by thinking about the people we like or dislike and then test the theory ourselves. Working hard to be that person who inspires others is great, but always try to be down to earth and friendly at the same time in order to connect with people. Practising building a rapport may take time, but it can often be a fun exercise too. It's not about being manipulative or trying to play *Jedi mind tricks* on someone, it's about developing the ability to interact with others in order to hopefully bring out the best in them.

5. Compliment them

It doesn't matter whether it's the first date or you've been together for fifty years, everyone likes receiving a compliment. A compliment in any situation is nice, but if you've spent time and effort preparing for a date, a compliment referring to your appearance would confirm your efforts have been appreciated. If a lady has been struggling to decide whether to wear the black dress or the red dress for the last two hours, complimenting her on her pretty dress would likely go down well. Obviously, if you hate the dress, you don't need to pretend you like it, just focus instead on something different that you do like. Telling someone you hate their dress on the first date, or any date for that matter, might not be the best move if you're hoping to see them again.

If someone is doing judo for the first time, and they're struggling to do a forward roll, for example, I wouldn't say "Hmm...that forward roll needs a lot of work". It could be the worst forward roll I've ever seen, but I'd be far more likely to say "Don't worry that's a good effort...I used to struggle with rolls when I first started". If later, they did something particularly well, I'd make a point of saying how good it was, often so others in the group (or parents) could hear. It's not just a case of being a good salesman, it's about building someone's confidence to help them later.

The same would be true on a first date. A compliment about a dress would definitely help them feel more comfortable, but a compliment about someone's smile, or laugh, or humour, or natural beauty, would really help to build their confidence, resulting hopefully in a more successful date.

6. Ask questions

Asking questions on a date is definitely a good way to find out more about the person, while at the same time allowing them to feel special and enjoy talking about their hobbies or passions. Make sure you're listening to the answers so you can expand with further questions on the subject or refer to them at a later date. Pick up on anything you have in common as that can strengthen the rapport between you.

7. Touching

By touching, I'm not talking about *touching them up*. I know we're talking about dating here, but touching can be used in many ways to build a rapport with someone and it doesn't necessarily have to be in a flirty way. Many straight men use touch to build a rapport with other straight men by shaking hands, for example, gripping someone's shoulder or patting them on the back.

The amount or type of touching on a date usually depends on how well you know one another at that point and if you're meeting for the first time on a blind date, for instance, you may need to tread carefully. Too much touching could make your date feel very uncomfortable, whereas no touching at all may come across slightly cold. I can't tell you how much or how little to touch your date, as it'll be down to you to gauge at the time. The reason I can't make the decision is because what's comfortable for one person may be totally unacceptable for another.

Going for a full-on cuddle or kiss in the first few minutes and hoping you avoid a knee to the groin or a smack in the face is probably not the way to go. Maybe a subtle hand on the back to usher them towards a car or a touch of the hand to thank them for the flowers/bottle of wine may be more appropriate. Take notice of their reaction to this first touch. If they're particularly tactile they may return it with a similar touch of their own, possibly giving you the green light to touch them again later. Each touch may become more intimate as the date progresses, but with each touch, you need to make an assessment of their reaction. If they flinch or move away, it's a good sign you've overstepped the mark and you may need to cool things slightly. Picking up on those signals could make the difference between a successful date and a disastrous one.

8. Humour

If you ask most people to name three other people, they'd choose to share a desert island with, it's likely that the majority would include at least one comedian. Not all of us are gifted with the quick wit of a comedian but most of us enjoy laughing, so sharing a joke or teasing one another usually helps to build rapport. Constantly making jokes at the other person's expense would almost certainly have the opposite effect, however, so be aware not to overstep the mark. On the other hand, having the confidence to laugh at yourself is actually a very attractive quality and those who struggle to take a joke are often very insecure.

9. Leave a lasting impression

First impressions are obviously important but finishing the date on a good note is probably where it really counts. Again, it's not for me to say what you should or shouldn't do, but as a rule, taking things slow can often leave the other person wanting more. Having said that, if you wish to see them again you need to make it clear, so they don't feel rejected. Sometimes if we're receiving mixed signals, we may end a date feeling confused. Asking them back to your place may be too forward if it's the first date, whereas an abrupt goodbye with no suggestion to meet up again may blow a successful evening. A good strategy may be to text your date to see if they arrived home safely. This obviously shows you care, but at the same time, it's then easy to continue the conversation by thanking them for a lovely evening and possibly making further arrangements.

Human dynamics coach, Matthew Hussey, is someone with far more knowledge on this subject than me and specialises in coaching women to find and keep the right man. I first saw him as a guest on the daytime television show *'Loose Women'* a few years ago, and he impressed me a lot. I wasn't particularly watching the show and I'd never heard of him, but he caught my attention right away. Everything this man said made perfect sense to me, and I could tell he was extremely switched on and mature beyond his years. I think he was about twenty-six at the time because I remember him mentioning he'd been coaching women for ten years and the Loose Women on the panel scoffed at the thought of being advised by a sixteen-year-old. Remaining completely cool, he informed them age had nothing to do with wisdom, and people who have been dating for many years repeat the same mistakes over and over. Again, they tried to suggest in the real world, women had too many things to do, such as cook, clean and look after children to have time to put his ideas into practise. Hussey rightly suggested these were simply excuses, which they were clearly not keen on hearing. It was probably no coincidence that most, if not all the Loose Ladies had been through separations and divorce.

From that point on, I started looking him up on the internet, not for dating advice of course, but I loved the guy's attitude to life, and I have taken on board some of his ideas to use in my own relationship.

PARTNERSHIPS AND MARRIAGE

12th December 2008

I looked into the eyes of the man staring back at me from my parent's bathroom mirror and took a deep breath. This was it – one of the most important days of my life. I flicked my hair about and wished I'd had it cut, as it really wasn't looking great. I fiddled with the collar on my suit, but no matter what I did, it wouldn't feel any more comfortable.

Like probably every bride or groom on their wedding day, I felt extremely nervous, but not for the reasons you're probably thinking of.

I was nervous about my hair looking rubbish on the photos I'd have to look back on for years to come, I was nervous about looking uncomfortable in my suit and making it obvious I'd spent my life wearing tracksuits and judo suits, I was nervous I'd skid in the ridiculously slippery shoes I was wearing, I was nervous I'd fluff my lines during the ceremony, I was nervous the rain might spoil things slightly, and I was nervous for Claire and hoped she was feeling okay. There were many things I was nervous about that day, but the only thing I wasn't nervous about was whether it was the right decision. We'd been together twelve years at this point, and we'd been engaged since 2001. We'd spoken about this day numerous times and it was something we both wanted.

By this stage, we already had Ryan and Joshua, and we'd already lived together for a number of years, so the commitment was already there. For me personally, getting married was just to make things more official, so everyone else took us more seriously, and we'd all finally share the same surname making our family seem more complete.

To this day, if someone asks me how long I've been married I have to stop and think about it, whereas if someone asks how long we've been together I can answer immediately.

A few years ago, I lost my wedding ring while playing with the kids on the beach and I've never felt the need to replace it. It's not that I see my marriage as unimportant, it's the fact that a piece of paper or a ring means very little to me. It's our actions within the marriage that count.

I remember going to a friend's wedding years ago, where everything was perfect. The bride looked like a princess, the venue was amazing, the food was fantastic, the weather was warm but not too hot and everything went like clockwork. There was one problem though – the relationship. Within six months the pair had separated and divorced soon afterwards.

On our wedding day, I was 110% certain it would last forever, and I feel no different today. I find it strange those who are in rocky relationships sometimes believe getting married or even having children will somehow strengthen things.

An old friend of mine used to cheat on his girlfriends all the time, but he assured me that once he got married and had children, his bad behaviour would stop. He *is married with children now, but we live in different parts of the country so unfortunately,* I can't confirm whether he kept his word or not.

I think a lot of people are afraid of the commitment as they feel a marriage means they'll need to change their behaviour. Claire obviously had to change her name, but for me personally nothing at all changed, except for maybe feeling slightly more grown-up.

Very often Claire and I are told we're the perfect couple and to a certain extent I believe they're right, but not in the way everyone thinks. We disagree on several things, we argue, we annoy each other with our bad habits, but we have an understanding I think many people fail to have. We both work at our marriage and realise it isn't meant to be perfect. We love the good things about one another, but we accept the bad, and no matter what, we appreciate the person we've agreed to spend the rest of our lives with.

So again, trying to stick to some basic rules will help us to strengthen our relationship, whether we're a new couple, in a long-term partnership, or in a marriage.

1. Be best friends

I'm not saying Dave from the pub, or Karen from bingo can't be considered your best friend and I'm definitely not suggesting you dump a friend you've known all your life when Mr/Mrs Right comes along. It's important to have those friends, but when we commit to a relationship and especially when that involves living together, I believe we should want to be with that person more than anyone else on the planet because after all, this is the person we'll be spending the most time with. I understand this doesn't always happen from day one, so that's why I think it's important not to rush into things. The fact that myself and Claire were both young at the beginning of our relationship probably helped us in the long run because we were forced to take each step slowly.

2. If we don't have trust, honesty, loyalty and respect, we have nothing

If we're hoping for a long and happy relationship, trust, honesty, loyalty and respect are not just important, but essential in my opinion. A loss or a lack of trust is probably the most common reason relationships fail. In my experience, those who are least trusting of their partners are usually the ones who are dishonest and out cheating themselves, although this may not be true in every case.

If you have a history of cheating on previous partners, you may make the excuse that, *"it was just a bit of fun"* or *"it was nothing serious"* or *"it was only sex"*. Now imagine the person you love doing exactly the same thing – is it just a bit of fun now?

The other classic lines are *"I just made a mistake"* or *"I was drunk"*, which are poor attempts to excuse the behaviour.

The truth is, we all know the consequences of cheating on a spouse or partner. If we haven't experienced it first-hand, we've seen the devastation it perhaps caused a friend, another family member, or a colleague. We see it everywhere: in newspapers, magazines, on TV, films and social media and the result is always the same.

We need to make the right choices to prevent ourselves from going down that road in the first place.

Checking our partner's phone messages or emails to make sure they're following the same code as us, is a complete lack of trust and if they're going to be dishonest or disloyal it'll happen regardless. Claire and I have always been comfortable swapping phones or having access to one another's messages and passwords. If you've got nothing to hide, there shouldn't be a problem.

Trust, honesty and loyalty don't just refer to fidelity. When we live together or spend most of our time with someone, it's inevitable from time to time we will irritate, frustrate or even anger one another. Communicating how we feel in an honest way without being hurtful or cruel can often prevent problems from escalating later.

Claire and I are very similar when it comes to our views and values, but our personalities are completely opposite. Claire is a very happy and positive person, although it doesn't take much for her to become annoyed or frustrated and her fiery temper can surface in an instant. Fortunately, she can return to normal quickly, almost as though nothing even happened.

If something bothers me, I'm far more likely to let it go. When I say *let it go*, I just mean I don't say anything. Inside it's still there and I haven't '*let it go*'. To everybody else, this may look as though I'm easier going than Claire as nothing much appears to bother me. However, as every irritation gets stored inside along with the last thing, gradually my patience starts to wear thin. Eventually, something small will trigger it, like a balloon bursting suddenly. Very few people have seen me mad or even annoyed, but when I finally release the frustration inside, the lot comes out at once. In arguments, I've been known to bring up issues from months before which are often nothing to do with the current problem, but it's my way of venting everything in one go.

Probably neither personality is ideal, and over the years, we've gradually become slightly more like one another, and we meet more in the middle. Nowadays, Claire's far more likely to bite her tongue until there's a more appropriate time to discuss something and I'm far more likely to bring up any issues I have early on, but in a calm and controlled way.

Our ability to communicate honestly and work as a team has increased our loyalty to one another, and we fully trust the other's commitment to the relationship. As we grow older together, our mutual love and respect grow stronger.

3. Give them freedom

It's natural to want to keep the person we love most to ourselves, but just like with our children, we must allow them freedom in order for them to grow as people, which is one of our basic human needs and one of the things that contribute most to our happiness.

Claire has always been a very sociable person and although she loves spending time with me and the kids, she also enjoys meeting up with friends. She has a close circle of friends that she's known for a lot of years, and they often meet up with the kids, eat out in restaurants, go to concerts and occasionally go out on the town in the evening.

I've never had a problem with this, just as she has no problem with me doing the same. In fact, she tries to encourage me to go out with friends or my brother as often as possible because I spend most of my time working or training in the evenings.

Don't get me wrong, we love spending time together, either alone or with our kids, but we appreciate that it's unhealthy to live in each other's pockets.

We've seen so many of our friends on both sides split up with husbands/wives/partners, and possessiveness has often been a contributing factor.

It amazes me how many adults rush home from training because they're worried about getting into trouble for being late and I've lost several members in the past because their partner isn't happy with them attending. Claire has mentioned about friends feeling uncomfortable being out or constantly checking the time, as they've got to be in at a certain time.

It's so important to allow them to live their life how they wish to and not try to control what they do, who they see and when they see them. Again, we need to see things from their perspective, if we hate being told what to do by our partners, don't do it to them. They're far more likely to give us freedom if we're happy for them to have freedom as well.

4. Don't expect perfection

None of us are perfect and there's no point making that our goal, as it's completely unattainable. A perfectionist will never be happy and will constantly look to improve, no matter what.

Expecting our partners to be perfect is again, completely unrealistic and if that's what we're looking for, we'll always be disappointed.

Accepting our partner the way they are is important. Don't try to change them as this very rarely works. Influencing them to change by behaving in a certain way, is far more likely to have an impact than telling them what they should and shouldn't be doing. Trying to force someone to behave differently will nearly always end in tears, we must embrace their flaws as well.

There are things about Claire I'm probably not very fond of, but if I were to remove some of them, I'm sure in a strange way I'd miss them, as those flaws are all part of her character – the person I fell in love with.

6. The grass is never greener

I've always believed in the quote *"the grass is never greener on the other side"*, and more recently I've seen an updated version *"if the grass is greener on the other side it's probably fake"*.

I think being grateful for what we have is one of the main elements of happiness, which applies to every area of our lives.

If you're in a long term relationship or a marriage, for the next minute or so, I want you to remember a time when your wife/husband/partner took your breath away, or gave you butterflies, or made you feel loved, happy or excited. Keep that picture in your mind and play that memory as many times as it takes to feel what you felt then.

Now, think of a person you've always fancied; your dream man or woman. It could be a celebrity, it could be your boss at work, it could be that guy from the gym you've never spoken to, it could be a neighbour, it could even be your plumber or local barmaid. If there's someone other than your partner you have the hots for, think of them right now...on the toilet! Not only that — imagine they've had a dodgy curry the night before, and they're letting it go big style.

It may be watching them poo doesn't necessarily bother you, so think of something that makes your stomach turn, like them picking their nose or biting their toenails. For me, it would have to be someone with half a jar of Marmite around their face trying to kiss me.

With a long-term partner, we've seen the best of them many times and possibly the butterfly feeling no longer happens, or maybe not in the same way.

The problem is we've seen the worst of them many times too, probably doing something I've already described or maybe even worse. What we fail to realise is that anybody we were with for a long period would inevitably show a side of themselves we found completely off-putting, and this needs to be kept in mind the next time we feel we can do better.

7. Don't get jealous when your partner receives attention

My wife Claire has long blond hair, blue eyes, she's slim, pretty, and I fancy her a lot! So why would I get annoyed at others for thinking the same thing? Surely it just means I've got good taste. To me it's a compliment when I see drivers rubbernecking out of their windows, or when blokes blatantly check her out at the beach, the pool or at a party. The reason it doesn't bother me is that they would love to be in my position and it's me who gets to go home with her at the end of the day, so why would I be worried?

Even when Claire goes out on a girl's night, it doesn't worry me, because again at the end of the night she comes home to me. She often tells me about guys asking for her number, or asking her to dance, but she's telling me this while lying next to me in bed, so why should I be worried? I know it'll happen because it does when I'm there, but again it comes down to trust.

I find it strange when I hear about a jealous partner trying to stop their other half from going out as they don't fully trust them. Surely that's got to be counterproductive?

In my opinion, our partner is far less likely to cheat on us if they believe they've got the best option already but putting restrictions on them is unlikely to convince them of that.

8. Make an effort

When a marriage or relationship ends, we often hear the couple just drifted apart, as though it was nobody's fault. In most cases *just drifted apart* should really be replaced with *stopped making an effort*, because that's actually a more accurate description of what's happened.

Most of us are guilty of making more effort for strangers than those we're closest to, but it's a good idea to remember how much effort we made for our partners at the beginning of the relationship and try as hard as we can not to let it slip. Remember how we tried to impress them and how nothing was too much trouble. Bringing them a cup of tea in bed first thing in the morning may once have been a pleasure, but ten years down the line it's easy to see things differently. Making the effort to leave a warm bed when he/she gets to lie-in AGAIN can become irritating, especially when it's now just expected. If we think about it though, nothing has changed, except for our attitude towards it.

Usually, the thing that slips along with our attitude is our appearance. Gaining weight once we're married or living with a partner is extremely common, often because we become too comfortable with the relationship and begin to take it for granted.

It's important to point out that gaining weight is not always a bad thing, as there could be a situation where someone has suffered from an eating disorder for example and a loving and supportive partner has encouraged them to gain weight in order to feel healthier and happy. There may also be a situation where a person is attracted to a larger partner and believes bigger is better. In these situations, gaining weight is okay.

We tend to see cracks in a relationship when one or both parties gain weight, although strangely enough, being big is generally not the problem. If we love someone, it doesn't usually matter how they look. Claire is slim and pretty and although this may have been a reason for the attraction initially, it's not the reason I love her today. If she was a size 16 rather than a size six, nothing would change, because she always makes an effort in our relationship. However, gaining weight usually represents a lack of effort and even slight laziness, so this is where the problem can occur.

The way we dress and present ourselves can often slip as well. At the beginning of a relationship, it's likely we wear clothes that flatter us and often ladies will wear makeup. Again, when we begin to take the relationship for granted, we're more likely to live in baggy t-shirts and joggers which are less flattering. This may lead to less attention from the partner followed by a feeling of rejection or neglect. This makes a person even less inclined to dress up, followed by even less attention, and the downward spiral continues.

Don't get me wrong, I'm not expecting Claire to tart herself up every day like she's some kind of trophy wife. In fact, if she did, I would be concerned about her insecurities, plus there'd be nothing different to look forward to when we went out for example. It's almost a running joke in our house how Claire whacks on the Pjs the second she comes through the door, but I kind of like that. If I forever saw her in the same a pair of baggy bottoms and an old t-shirt with ketchup down the front, it would suggest a lack of effort, but Claire wears different types of pyjamas depending on her mood or the temperature. She has warm ones, short ones, baggy ones, tight-fitting ones, cute ones and even sexy ones, yet she looks good in all of them.

When we go out, she'll make a lot of effort to look nice, and I always feel proud to be with her, although she's never been one for wearing heavy makeup. If some ladies remove all their makeup it can be a bit of a shock because they look so different, whereas Claire will sometimes say "I'm not wearing any makeup, do I look okay to go to (wherever)?" Most of the time I haven't even noticed she isn't wearing any until she mentions it. That's not to say that she doesn't ever bother, as she'll wear mascara and have her toes painted most of the time.

9. Be present

Making an effort isn't just about how we look; it's about how we interact with one another on a daily basis as well.

These days it's common for people to work long hours and when we arrive home it's very easy to get distracted by our phones, computers, games consoles, the TV, or maybe even work that's been brought home. It seems chatting and laughing about our day around the family dinner table is a thing of the past.

For most people, the day starts with the morning rush to get to work (and school, for those with children) meaning there's very little interaction except for a few yawns, grunts and maybe a brief "goodbye" on the way out.

After work, they return home and say a quick *"hello"* to the other half (if they're lucky). There's no point in them saying *"hello"* to the kids because there'll be no response anyway. They chuck a ready meal in the microwave before parking themselves on the sofa and eating it from their lap. They switch on one screen or another and remain in their virtual world until it's time for bed. Often the distractions prevent them from going to bed at a reasonable time, resulting in little or no bedtime interaction before they nod off. Come morning, the rush starts again, and the cycle continues.

It all sounds quite sad, but how many people are reading this thinking "that sounds like my life". The truth is, we become comfortable in our relationships and bad habits begin to form. Even when people go out, they struggle to break the same pattern. How many times do we see couples in a restaurant, both on their phones without any interaction across the table?

I've heard that people play a game in restaurants where the person who picks up their phone first pays the bill. It sounds like a good incentive to stay off our phones, but why would we need an incentive to interact with our partner when we should want to more than anything else?

If this sounds like you and your partner, you may need to discuss what needs to change and make a pact together to improve the relationship and rekindle the old spark you once had between you. It may be difficult to break the old habits initially, but if you work as a team it may actually be a lot of fun.

10. Don't try to change them

Trying to change our partner's behaviour just by telling them to change is very unlikely to work, especially if they were like that at the beginning of the relationship. We're more likely to get a result if we either lead by example or explain the benefits of them changing their behaviour. If they're dead against changing, we sometimes have to accept them for who they are and just focus instead on all the things we love about them.

11. Find common interests

Meeting our future partner while doing a hobby we enjoy is usually the ideal scenario, as it gives us this common interest from the word go. As you know, judo was the common interest between me and Claire, but despite us being young and different ages, it allowed us to form a friendship in the early stages, which led to a relationship later on. Even though Claire no longer participates in judo, she's still active and enjoys keeping fit and healthy. Our children now do judo as well as other physical activities which have included football, gymnastics, swimming, and ballet.

We share many interests and enjoy walking, eating out, cinema, cosy nights in watching films, and we've even been known to play board games and occasionally the kids' Xbox.

We enjoy each other's company, but we don't feel the need to live in one another's pockets either. We understand that it's good to have our own hobbies too, and we've always encouraged the other with whatever they decide to do.

12. Show we care

To love someone can be quite easy, but to show we care generally takes more effort and is often the thing that disappears in a relationship. Telling our partner that they look nice, or giving them a peck on the cheek when we arrive home, a cuddle when we wake up, or even a text message to ask how their day is going, may all seem like small things, but in terms of keeping a relationship alive they are actually big things. Everyone likes a compliment and to know someone cares for them. If we love someone, we need to let them know daily and not just when we want something in return.

It's not particularly difficult to do these things and making a tiny bit more effort can help a relationship enormously.

13. Date nights

Regardless of how long we've been together, whether we work long hours, if we have kids, or we're struggling for money, date nights are so important (daytime dates count too).

Making time for our partners again shows we care for them, as well as giving us both something to look forward to.

If you have children, try to arrange childcare for the evening, or make the most of the opportunity when they're sleeping over at their friend's houses.

If money's an issue, still make the effort. Maybe treat yourselves to some fish and chips and sit by the seaside or in the park, or even just chat in the car.

Even taking a walk together can remind us of why we're with that person, there's no need to go to fancy restaurants every time.

14. Compromise

No matter how strong a relationship is, there'll always be disagreements along the way, regarding our decisions and beliefs. Communication is the best way to resolve our differences, although we need to under-stand it's not always possible to get everyone to think the way we do. Occasionally, we need to compromise and meet in the middle, which usually keeps both parties happy.

We may be lucky enough to share hobbies and interests, but they are likely to enjoy things that we find mind-numbingly boring as well. Likewise, they may believe strongly in something we find difficult to agree with. Arguing about things rarely convinces the other person to change their opinion, so explaining your view on a subject while having respect for their view, usually allows both parties to find a compromise.

In terms of interests, a compromise is simple. Within my own relationship, the things we both enjoy, such as going to the cinema, walking and eating out, we'll do together. I enjoy watching or going to big sporting events, while Claire prefers watching or going to concerts or musicals, so we tend to do those with friends, because we know the other is less interested. However, there have been times when we've accompa-nied one another to an event that only the other enjoys. In this situation, it would be easy to be grumpy for the duration in protest at being dragged along, but on each occasion, we've found it possible to enjoy the time together.

Why?

Because we can feel good about being unselfish and get enormous pleasure out of seeing the other happy.

In fact, despite musicals not being my cup of tea, I was surprised to really enjoy myself when we watched '*The Sound of Music*' together and I even volunteered to watch another one at a later date.

15. Be spontaneous

Tony Robbins, the world's leading Life Strategist, often talks about the six human needs that are required to make us happy and fulfilled. These are **certainty, uncertainty, significance, love/connection, growth** and **contribution**.

These needs are also true within a relationship. If we look at the first two needs, **certainty** and **uncertainty**, we'll see they contradict one another.

What we must realise is we need both simultaneously in order to keep the relationship alive. We probably know couples who have one without the other and the result is the relationship breaks down unless changes are made.

To clarify briefly what I mean, there are those couples who:

1. Appear to have the perfect relationship, often over a long period; they fall in love, enjoy each other's company, make each other laugh, both want to marry and have children and have similar interests. Then one day (often after marriage and having children) they announce they're separating, and nobody can believe it.

2. Have a relationship full of fun and passion and although both parties seem to love being together, one

or both fail to commit fully to the relationship leading to a separation.

Relationship one is an example of certainty without uncertainty, and relationship two is an example of uncertainty without certainty.

Relationship one had certainty and uncertainty in the early stages, but as the commitment grows stronger (the certainty), the excitement (the uncertainty) begins to disappear, until both are so locked into the routine of life, it becomes boring to the point of unhappiness and the feeling of being trapped. Often couples live in this situation for years before they either split or make a change.

Relationship two is full of excitement (or uncertainty) from beginning to end, but as one or both fails to ever commit (certainty) the relationship is unable to progress to the next level.

So, how can we guarantee to have both certainty and uncertainty within the relationship?

Combine the good elements from relationship one and relationship two and, we should be on to a winner. If on top of that, we make our partner feel special in the relationship, they're bound to feel significant and loved, allowing the relationship to grow over time. If we do that, we've covered five out of the six human needs and it then puts us in a great position to do what I'm doing right now, and cover need six – contributing my knowledge in order to help other couples.

If you've got certainty in your relationship and things are becoming slightly routine, it's time to rekindle that uncertainty, or if you need me to spell it out – the *spontaneity*.

_____

If you've got certainty in your relationship and things are becoming slightly routine, it's time to rekindle that uncertainty, or if you need me to spell it out – the **spontaneity**.

There are many ways to be spontaneous in order to spice up a relationship. I won't tell you what you should or shouldn't do to be spontaneous as that's for you to figure out, but you need to be able to keep your partner guessing. People like the thought of being spontaneous, but they often stop themselves because it conflicts with their personality. I can relate to this slightly and I'll explain why.

16. Have different personalities

For a long time, I struggled to figure out exactly who I was and sometimes I was unsure if I was being *the real me* or just acting to a certain extent.

As far back as I can remember I've always been quite shy and often used to struggle in certain areas because of it, particularly making phone calls to people I didn't know. I'm still not fond of it if I'm honest, but as a child, it used to petrify me. Some people who know me today will find that hard to believe, as it's the job of an athlete and coach to be confident, although it's still there to an extent.

So, due to my shyness, it often felt as though I was playing a character at times and I'd sometimes beat myself up over it because I was continuously trying to be someone I wasn't. I was also aware that this shy little boy was holding me back, so I had to change.

That's when it started to occur to me that we all need to change in order to develop and I realised these different characters were, in fact, me after all.

We hear people say the best thing to do is to *'just be yourself'*. I found that difficult in my younger days because I wasn't sure who *the real me* actually was and it possibly held me back at times. I realise now we can be whoever we want to be and it's okay to bring out whatever character is required at that particular time.

Often people talk about having an angel on one shoulder and a devil on the other, suggesting they have a good side and a bad side, like a split personality. I think I have a few personalities that are required for the different areas of my life and I'm now very comfortable switching whenever I need to. This may sound familiar to you too and I'm sure it's very common. I believe only having one personality will work in certain areas of our lives but not in others, being able to call on other personalities in different situations can help us immensely.

These personality changes are helpful in a relationship and we shouldn't feel bad about it. For instance, it's a good thing to be the responsible grown up while sorting out our finances, but who wants that person around at a party? We might be a hard working person but being chilled and relaxed at home is okay. There's also nothing wrong with being Mumsy on the school run, excitable at the theme park, childish at the kid's playground, or sexy in the bedroom. Even being that shy vulnerable kid is okay from time to time as well.

17. Say sorry and forgive

Like many kids at school, I learnt about The First World War during history lessons. Hearing about the battles that took place was interesting to me and I used to wonder what it would feel like to be part of it, trapped in a war where two out of three men died during the fighting and many more from disease. Ultimately, millions were killed, but one of the facts that used to baffle me most was why it all started. I know Archduke Franz Ferdinand was assassinated in Sarajevo in 1914, but I'm still clueless to this day, quite how everything escalated in the way it did.

On a much smaller scale, that's pretty much the pattern with most arguments we have; something triggers it, it escalates out of control and before we know it we've forgotten exactly how and why it all started, but the focus shifts to winning the argument as opposed to resolving the problem.

I mentioned earlier how Claire was far more likely to provoke an argument but finds it easier to apologise than I would. She would've moved on while I would be replaying it in my mind. I've always hated injustice, so if I think I've been treated unfairly I often feel it needs to be rectified.

We still argue on occasions which I think is healthy for any relationship, but these days I'm a lot more likely to apologise regardless of how the argument starts. *'It takes two to tango'* as they say and an apology from me for my part in the argument, more often than not leads to Claire doing the same.

We always try to put things into perspective, and we have no doubts about our love for one another and our commitment to the relationship. This means even while an argument is taking place, we realise we both still love one another, and we understand it may have started due to frustration, a misunderstanding, or even just tiredness, which prevents it from escalating to the point of no return.

Swallowing our pride is all it takes and it's difficult to stay mad at someone who isn't mad with us. Trying to be the bigger person and being the first to apologise is positive for the relationship if we're sure our partner had no real bad intentions. *'Sorry'*s small word, but it makes a huge difference within a relationship. In fact, if everyone used it more often, the world could become a far happier place.

SEX

I better make this first sentence good, because I wouldn't mind betting many of you have turned to this page first...

...and now you're smiling because I guessed right!

Sex is one of those subjects many people get offended by or embarrassed about, but in a book about happiness, it simply must be included as it makes many people extremely happy.

For a start, it's essential for our survival as a species, so love it or hate it, there's no getting away from it.

Throughout most sections of this book, I refer to my own life in relation to the subject, but as my readers may include my parents, Claire's parents, and possibly even my children, it may be better not to make any personal references. So, for the rest of this section, I'll talk about the subject in a slightly **more general way if you don't mind.**

Another reason to be more general is the fact there are so many opinions about sex in terms of what's good and what's not good, and what's acceptable and what's not acceptable. This means what works or feels good for one person, may be a complete turn off for another, so there are no right or wrong answers when it comes to sex necessarily.

Just like with everything else I've talked about in this book, I don't consider myself to be an expert and there's no way I'm going to attempt to give out any technical advice. However, just like with our previous subjects, I believe there are still some general rules that may help those who are either new to sex or struggling with it in some way.

1. It's all in the head

Many people believe being successful between the sheets (or any other location for that matter), is largely due to the size of the equipment and a few slick moves. This could be that we refer to a couple participating in sex as *getting physical*. What most people tend to forget is the brain is in fact the largest and most sensitive sex organ in the body, and although size and a slick move or two may play a part in fulfilling sex, they are unlikely to make an impact unless the brain is engaged in the correct way first. In other words, if we can't turn our partner on mentally, then the chance of them achieving sexual fulfilment is extremely unlikely.

Just pouncing on your partner without any warning is likely to result in rejection, which in turn may lead to an argument. You may wonder why your partner never wants sex and the more it happens the more you convince yourself your partner has lost interest, resulting in less effort on your part. This pattern produces a downward spiral until a sexual relationship is almost non-existent and just like with exercise, the less you do the less you want to do.

This type of pattern is common in relationships, but often all that's missing is the engagement of the partner's brain. The *pouncer* has almost certainly engaged their own mind prior to the pouncing, with their own sexual arousal building over time. The person being *pounced upon* is unlikely to be feeling any sexual arousal at all and if they're occupied with something else it may well be the last thing on their mind. The following examples are scenarios that may occur when only one of us is engaged mentally:

Example one: You're in the kitchen doing a few jobs and you look out of the window to see your husband/ partner working hard in the garden. It's a hot day, and he's taken off his shirt, which you love. It's summer, so he has a lovely tan and the sweat and dust just increase your desire. As you look on, imagining everything you'd like to do to him right now, he accidentally hits his thumb with the hammer. He holds his thumb tight and grits his teeth before making his way towards the house. This is your chance to play the role of a naughty nurse and to help his pain go away, but what you've got in your head doesn't quite go according to plan. As he enters the house you laugh playfully and attempt to kiss his thumb better, which annoys him straight away. As he runs it under the cold tap you hug around his naked torso, and he complains that he's sweaty and smelly and needs a shower. You tell him you don't care, you're drawn towards his manly aroma, yet he abruptly shrugs you off telling you that he's hot, tired and dehydrated and needs to get on in the garden.

Example two: It's Monday afternoon and you're feeling happy because the boss has unexpectedly given you the rest of the day off. Hopefully, your wife/partner will be in when you return home because you may get a chance to spend some adult time together before the school run. You picture what she was wearing that morning; the black leggings which she keeps talking about throwing away. The last time she took them off she was about to bin them, but you talked her into keeping them. You think she looks hot in them and you have no idea what she means when she says they make her look fat.

On the drive home, you imagine your wife's surprise when you walk through the door early and you plan to make the most of it by whisking her up to the bedroom.

You arrive home but her car's not there, so you decide to ring her – no answer.

You text instead and have just about given up hope when you receive a text back – *"Now cummin"*.

You hope there's a double meaning to that text, so you quickly jump in the shower to freshen up.

You get out of the shower just in time to hear the front door open, followed by plastic bags rustling and tins crashing onto the floor. You're more or less dry so you decide to walk downstairs to greet your wife with the towel wrapped around your waist – *that should get her going.* She almost bumps into you in the hallway as she stumbles through the door once more, carrying several shopping bags in each hand while holding her purse tightly under her chin.

You go to kiss her, and she tuts... *"grabbing some bags would be a lot more helpful!"*

You chuckle in order to lighten the mood and this appears to irritate her even more.

She walks through to the kitchen and begins pulling stuff from the bags, but instead of helping out, you stand mesmerised by her shapely behind appearing from beneath her coat.

You walk up behind her and place your hands on her hips, but she pulls away sharply, *"you always grab my wobbly bits!"* she snaps.

You attempt once again to soften the blow, *"you're so sexy when you're angry,"* you answer, flashing your best smile.

She scowls once more.

"Get upstairs and get ready you pervert! If you want some tea tonight, I suggest you make yourself useful for a change and go pick the kids up."

Hmm...not quite like the movies, is it?

But despite these being made up scenarios, I'm sure many of you can relate to them. The issue with both scenarios is that only one person has engaged their *sexual brain*, while the other is caught completely in the wrong state.

To engage your partner's sexual brain, it's important to have initiated some kind of mental foreplay. This is not to be confused with physical foreplay, which often involves kissing, cuddling and touching one another. Mental foreplay in our first scenario may have been a text to say: *I'm watching you from the kitchen window and let's just say the weather's not the only thing that's hot today babe! Maybe we can cool off in the shower? xxxx.*

At the very least, a wolf whistle out of the kitchen window may have sown the seed.

Mental foreplay with the second scenario may be slightly more difficult because being given the afternoon off was unexpected, plus the wife wasn't present, or in the correct state on her return home. Maybe a text before leaving work suggesting your intentions for the afternoon may have helped, which at least gives her more time to come around to the idea and possibly start to conjure up scenarios in her own head. These thoughts are likely to alter her emotional and physiological state, which in turn is likely to result in a more positive outcome. When both of you have engaged your sexual brains it's likely to result in fireworks, however, it's helpful to realise that being too obvious or following the same old routine can be frustrating or even off-putting for your partner.

2. Show you care
Engaging your partner in mental foreplay is a good idea before any kind of physical interaction as we've already mentioned, but if you only ever give them attention in order to initiate sex, your ability to get the desired response is likely to be short-lived. Regardless of whether your relationship is serious or not, nobody likes to feel used and abused (unless this is part of an agreed role-play).

You and your partner may enjoy rough animalistic sex as much as loving and caring sex, but either way, as long as love and care is displayed prior to, and more importantly afterwards, it doesn't matter *how you have sex*, because that is simply down to personal choice.

The type of sex that is practised is entirely up to those involved, but regardless of who does what to who and for how long, it's important for it to be fun for all parties, which comes through trust, understanding, communication and if you're lucky, love too.

Some of us will obviously be more connected with our partner than others, but if you want your sex life to be more fulfilling, it's more likely you'll achieve this outcome if you're always understanding and take the pressure off them to *perform*. This type of attitude takes the pressure off yourself too, which should allow you both to enjoy the experience.

I once heard a judo coach say *"Judo is like sex...you can't be brilliant all the time."*

It's worth remembering.

3. Have fun

As I've already mentioned, it's easier to have fun if you're under less pressure, which is a big advantage for couples that have been together for some time. Try not to make sex too serious, otherwise, you're far more likely to worry about everything needing to be perfect. It's important to be able to laugh at yourself, not just in bed, but in all situations, because unless it's in a film, things often do go wrong. So, go ahead and laugh, because falling off the bed, struggling to get that bra off, or a fart at the wrong moment, is all part of the fun.

If it's your partner on the other end of it, you *can* still laugh. A word of warning though — just be sure they know you're laughing along with them rather than at them. If you mention you've done something similar previously, or joke that their clumsiness is one of the things you find so attractive, it's far more likely to keep things on track.

4. Communicate

It's common to hear that communication is the key to great sex, but when we think about communication, we often only think in terms of verbal communication.

Many people feel awkward and embarrassed when it comes to talking about sex and never truly express what they like or dislike, even when they've been with someone for some time. You may be totally confident and clear about what you want, and you may feel comfortable simply asking your partner, but let's not forget there are many ways to communicate.

You don't need your partner to stick their thumb up during sex and say *"Yeah that's good!"*, or on the other hand give you a thumbs down accompanied by *"Nah, don't like that"*.

Instead, you need to notice signs such as:

- How are they breathing?
- How are they moving?
- Has their colour changed?
- Has their temperature changed?
- Has their expression changed?
- What noises are they making?
- How are they touching you?
- Do they appear comfortable?
- Does it feel right?

There are slightly more obvious signs we may be looking for of course, but I'm sure I don't need to spell those out to you.

Immediately afterwards look at their body language for positive signs:

- Are they smiling?
- Do they look content?
- Are they talking in a positive way?

Take on board any verbal feedback. If they say, *"that was fantastic!"* and it sounds genuine (not sarcastic), it's highly likely you've done a good job. If they say, *"it was good but..."*, maybe there's room for improvement. Don't get offended by honest feedback and don't let it affect your confidence, because it's knowledge that'll help you in the future. If someone's suggesting how you could improve, it's definitely a good sign and it's very likely they'd like to benefit from that improvement later on.

Just like with everything in life, we learn through watching, listening and then practising something. Whether the advice on a subject is coming from your boss at work, a colleague, a friend, a swimming coach, a martial arts instructor, or a sexual partner, it really makes no difference, because none of us are born with this knowledge. With time and experience, we generally become more confident just like with any other skill. Remember, if a sexual partner wants to get rid of you, why would they bother giving you advice on how to improve? A football manager isn't likely to give advice to a player they about to sell to another team.

When we talk about the importance of communication when it comes to sex, very often we think about the emotional and physical communication during the act. However, let's not forget that despite the fact sex is meant to be enjoyed, the consequences of sex at the wrong time or with the wrong person can affect the rest of our lives. Communicating whether you need to use contraception, whether you're underage, whether you have a sexually transmitted disease, or whether you already have a partner, should all be discussed long before the possibility of anything physical taking place. We're all human, and we all have urges, but those feelings can disappear within seconds. The consequences (and I don't need to tell you what those are), often destroy relationships, trust, dreams, health, and often they're gone forever!

5. Spice it up

This isn't where I suggest you dress head to toe in a rubber costume, suspend one another from the ceiling, or start to introduce other partners. If you already do that, everyone's in agreement and nobody gets hurt, who am I to say that it's wrong — if it's right for you, that's fine. However, what I am suggesting is no matter how much we enjoy routine, we also have a need for variety in our lives too. Even if your partner has told you that you were fantastic once before, it doesn't necessarily mean they'll want it in the same way, at the same time and in the same place every single time. I love a roast dinner, but if I had to eat it for every single meal for the rest of my life, I'd soon have less enthusiasm for roast dinners. Experimentation is good if you except you won't always hit the jackpot every time, but in doing so, you may find you like something even more than a roast dinner from time to time.

6. Compromise

If you remember, compromise was one of the rules I included in the partnerships/marriage section earlier in the book. In fact, a sexual relationship isn't that different from any other type of relationship in terms of the rules that'll maintain its success (compromise, consideration, care, communication to name a few). I would suggest that the happiest marriages are very likely to include happy sex lives too, as they just apply the same rules to that element of their relationship.

As there are so many ways to have sex, what are the chances you and your partner enjoy exactly the same things, done in exactly the same way, at exactly the same time?

I would say almost no chance.

Going back to the food analogy — If I love a roast dinner but Claire only ever serves up a chicken curry, I'm going to feel as though I'm never considered. Whereas, if she cooks a roast dinner every single time I want it and never gets to eat the chicken curry I know she loves, that's not going to make me feel great about myself.

The answer is obviously to have a chicken curry one night, followed by a roast dinner the next. On another night we may decide spaghetti Bolognese is a good option because we both love eating that and it's a change from the other two meals.

Now I realise this is turning into a cookery book as opposed to *'Fifty Shades of Grey'*, but I'm sure you understand the point I'm attempting to make.

CHILDREN

See what I did there?

A section on sex followed by a section on children, just as a reminder to those who are becoming too relaxed about contraception.

Becoming a parent should never be taken lightly. It's not something you should do half-heartedly and if you're unsure whether you want to be a parent, then perhaps the time isn't right for you yet. That's not to say you won't be apprehensive, if not petrified, even if you are ready.

For most of us, having children is one of the most (if not *the* most) fulfilling things we'll ever experience in our lives. We've all had our days when we may consider it to be the biggest mistake of our lives, but when it comes down to it, we know that's not generally the truth.

It's difficult to describe that moment when we become a parent for the first time. It's not easy to decide whether we've suddenly become either more, or less significant as a result. We know immediately we'd die for them, but on the other hand we'd do anything to survive for them too. It's a strange feeling to get your head around although I'm sure there are many of you who can completely relate to it.

At 10.52 am on the 2nd December 2005, Ryan was delivered, but not without some drama. It was a shoulder dystocia birth, which meant that Ryan's body remained trapped inside Claire with his shoulder caught beneath her pelvis. His head had emerged some time before and I watched the calm expression on the midwife's face gradually fade as it was replaced by signs of concern, followed by a controlled panic.

I became conscious of an alarm, seconds before a team of doctors and nurses entered the room like the SAS raiding a building. I was grappled to one side, as my head tried to process what was going on. I stood in shock for a few seconds, but it was obvious this wasn't in the script. As quickly as they'd entered, they were gone again, along with the lifeless, blue shape they were carrying.

I quickly gathered my thoughts only to realise we were momentarily alone. Straight away my concern was for Claire, and I grabbed her hand and told her everything would be okay. I had no idea whether it would be of course, and I was probably more frightened than I'd ever been in my life, but I just knew no matter what happened we'd get through it, even at that stage.

A short while later, maybe thirty seconds possibly, we heard the most beautiful sound ever — our baby son crying. The funny thing was, with all the drama we'd forgotten all about the sex of the baby and so had the doctors. Once he'd been placed into Claire's arms it was quite some time before we thought to look, although at that stage we really didn't care either way.

That was fourteen years ago but it still feels like yesterday. The feeling you get when you hold your child for the first time is truly magical. I remember holding all three of my children and being completely mesmerised by how perfect they were. In those moments, nothing else matters and it's impossible to ever imagine being angry, annoyed or disappointed with them (although we all know it's inevitable).

Those moments are often when we tell ourselves everything is going to change for the better, that our child will be awesome because we're going to be the best parent alive.

What we always seem to underestimate is that we're about to enter a world of shit...literally!

Yes, I am joking, but even so, I'm sure there are very few parents who would disagree that parenting is one of the toughest jobs known to man (and even women).

I once saw a video where a number of people applied for a job online and were filmed during their interviews. The position they'd applied for was *'Director of Operations'*. The job was fake, but the applicants had no idea.

The interviewer started by explaining about the position:

"It's so much more than just a job, it's probably the most important job — It's a job that requires standing up almost all the time, constantly on your feet, constantly bending over, constantly exerting yourself, a high level of stamina, basically twenty-four hours a day, seven days a week". He continued, "You can have lunch, but only when the associate has finished eating their lunch — the position requires excellent negotiation and interpersonal skills — the associate needs constant attention that may require staying up with them during the night — birthdays, Christmas, New Years and holidays, the workload is going to increase — oh, and there is no salary".

As the applicants stumble over their responses, disbelieving that a position like this even exists, the interviewer continues to sell it by saying the feeling they would receive from helping the associate would be immeasurable.

The applicants all ask why anyone would take the position and one even questions whether it's legal.

The interviewer smiles and tells them billions of people already hold the position currently, before revealing...

It's mums!

Their reactions are priceless, firstly due to being on the wrong end of a prank, but slowly it sinks in just how much they take their own mum for granted, which I think we all do to a certain extent. We all know it's a time-consuming and often thankless job, yet being a parent is also joyful, rewarding and fulfilling in so many ways and this is why we choose to do it.

As human beings we won't do anything unless there's something in it for ourselves, including being parents. We may help people all the time and not expect anything in return, or we may give money to charity on a regular basis without any thanks and without needing to broadcast it to the world, but what we get from it is a feeling of significance and satisfaction.

The feeling we get from being a parent is knowing a part of us will continue once we're gone — not just our name or even our genetics, but our influence. It's important to most parents that we pass on our beliefs to our children and encourage them to learn from our mistakes.

The big problem is, even as adults, and indeed parents, we still make a lot of mistakes. It's a job we've been doing for hundreds of thousands of years but it's a job that, to this day, nobody has mastered perfectly. We don't have all the answers, and even if we did, what are the chances of our children always listening to that advice?

I love being a parent and like to think I try my best in that role, but I'm no Supernanny. As with everything else, it's not for me to tell you how to do things, that's up to you to decide, but what I would suggest is work on the person you can control — *yourself.*

If you're the type of parent who tells their child to stop f***ing swearing, you've got a lot to learn, although I'm guessing you learnt it from your own parents also, which is unfortunate. If you haven't got any good role models yourself, you need to find some quick and practise the behaviours you expect from your children. Quite simply, you can't expect your children to tidy up after themselves if you're prepared to live in a pigsty.

Children don't need a boss, they need a leader, and the best ones are those who lead by example.

Children don't need a boss, they need a leader, and the best ones are those who lead by example. If we want to help our children become the best they can be, it's essential we become the best we can be beforehand.

A great analogy for this is if a plane gets into difficulties, we are told to fit our own oxygen mask and life vest before we fit them on our children. It has nothing to do with whom we consider more important (as almost all parents would put their children first), but it's a question of being far more capable of helping them once we've helped ourselves.

Knowing we've given our children the tools to cope with life is one of the most fulfilling parts of being a parent. My children are still quite young and are not yet ready to leave the nest, but they have acquired skills, knowledge and confidence from us that have brought them this far.

They've not just acquired this from us alone of course. They would've gained some of this from grandparents and other family members, teachers, friends, clubs they've attended, and from life experiences they've had up to this point.

This is the other problem — we're not in control of everything they learn and experience, meaning we need to prepare them to make decisions for themselves. We also need to understand that every decision won't be the right one (just as it isn't for us either), but we need to be reassured that life is about making mistakes and learning from them. If our children make mistakes it's not because we've failed as parents, it's just the normal process of life. That's not to say we should just leave them to their own devices either, because that's likely to lead to problems too.

Remember, we won't be the only leaders in our children's lives, and we need to consider that not all of them will have their best interests at heart. The worst-case scenario is that they may be targeted by a paedophile who may be a teacher or club leader for example, which is every parent's worst nightmare. We obviously need to educate them for them to recognise when these situations may be developing and not be afraid to speak up. In some ways though, these problems may be easier to rectify than a friend/friends who may be a bad influence on our children.

It's inevitable that at some point our children will interact or even become friendly with other children who are not to our liking. It's also inevitable that at some stage they'll be encouraged to do something they shouldn't, whether it be, smoke, drink, skip school, or steal something. It's impossible to monitor them 24/7 and nor should we want to, it's important for them to experience these pressures and to make the decisions for themselves. In my opinion, a child who is dictated to is far more likely to go off the rails at any opportunity. If you explain to a child why something may or may not be a good idea and then leave them to make the decision whether it is the correct one or not (unless they're putting themselves in danger), they are far more likely to come up with the correct answer.

However, if they don't, they'll learn the lesson for next time and grow in confidence as their decision making improves.

Showing them the right way, rather than telling them the right way, is a lot more effective than we realise. Our children are influenced by our behaviour all the time, and we need to be more aware of this. Driving is a great example. We assume our first driving lesson is with a driving instructor when we're adults, but in fact, it would've been several years previous to that when we first sat in the back seat of our parent's car. Watching a parent shout and swear at other road users, cut people up as they switch lanes, or tailgate just inches behind the car in front, is likely to make this type of behaviour behind the wheel seem acceptable. If *you're* that parent, it's worth giving it some thought, as you can hardly complain when your grown-up son or daughter wraps their car around a tree.

Strangely, one of the most common difficulties involving parenting is not always with the children. There's a good chance the parents in the child's life do not share the same view when it comes to parent-ing. Their personalities may blend perfectly within the partnership, but when it comes to raising a child, they may have a clash of styles that causes all sorts of friction between them. It's hardly surprising as we're all raised differently, but if your view is completely opposite to that of your partner, it's important for you both to discuss how you will come to a compromise.

Problems usually arise when one parent says one thing, and the other parent says the opposite. This gives the child no option but to take sides, causing friction between the parents and leaving one of them feeling undermined and disrespected. This can make the whole family feel uncomfortable, but what's even more of a problem, is that the parents encourage an opportunity for a child to play one off against another, later on, leading to further unrest within the family unit.

It's impossible to discuss every decision, but if one of you makes a decision that the other disagrees with, it should be spoken about at a later time. It would almost always be inappropriate to step in and try to overrule or even contradict the other parent's decision. Compromising on decisions, working together as a team and being consistent, is far more likely to produce the desired behaviour from your children, plus they will learn to conduct themselves correctly in the future, or even in their current relationships.

Being a parent is a tough job and it's a very important job, but it's one that can bring us so much joy and happiness if we do it correctly (but not perfectly). Be the person you'd like them to become but enjoy allowing them to grow into the person *they* wish to be too. You never know, it may be possible you like *that* person even more.

CHAPTER 4

PROGRESSION

TIME

Ask the average person to describe a *ball*, or a *cup*, or a *house*, and they'll be able to do it no problem. Even things that can't be seen, such as *the wind*, or even *love* are not particularly difficult to find a definition to. If we ask someone to describe *time* on the other hand, it's difficult for them to do so without actually using the word *time*.

We all instinctively understand the meaning of time, whether we can describe it or not, but we only really understand its value when we have far less of it.

In the days before mobile phones and tablets, I remember the boredom I felt sat in the doctor's waiting room, or on long car journeys and wishing for the time to vanish. An hour used to seem like a day as a child, and I, like so many others, would literally wish my life away.

I remember being at a particularly hard training camp in my late teens, and with weeks still to go, I sat with my friends attempting to work out how many seconds remained before we were due to return home. At the time I longed for those seconds to disappear, but each of those seconds helped to shape me into the man I am today.

As a person in my forties, time already seems far more precious than it did when I was a kid, although I probably have no idea how precious it is in comparison to a ninety-year-old, or someone with terminal cancer.

There's nothing more valuable than something that can't be bought, and *time* sits at the very top because without *time*, we have nothing.

I often wonder whether the ninety-year-old, or a person with a terminal illness are actually the lucky ones, because they know for certain they have little time left and appreciate every second. I may be forty-something and probably appreciate my time more than the average child, but if I died next week I may not have appreciated my time as much as I should have, as it's natural to assume we'll live into old age.

As difficult as it is sometimes, it's important to imagine every year, month, week, day, hour, minute and second as though it's our last. Only then can we use our time wisely and understand what's truly important.

Despite this, it's also important to realise life isn't a race either. Doing things at our own pace is going to make us far happier than competing against everybody else. We may look at others and believe we're in front or behind, but who says when things must be done?

Once upon a time, things would be done at a certain time and in a certain order. If a particular goal hadn't been achieved by a certain age, it was generally thought that the person had missed the boat. Nowadays we see people getting married at sixteen or sixty, they can educate themselves at six or one hundred and six, and starting a successful business is possible for a child or an old age pensioner.

We can get anything we want out of life when we start to make good decisions and use the time we have wisely. The excuse we use for not having what we want a lot of the time is, *"we haven't got the time"*.

I'm sure we've all said it at some point, but, *"I haven't got time"* is always a lie no matter whether we realise it or not. *"I haven't got time"* actually means, *"It's not my priority"*. We can always make time if we believe something is a priority.

Spending Christmas Day with our families would be the priority for most of us, hence few of us work on that day. A doctor or nurse sometimes must work because sick people are the priority. An Olympic athlete may train on Christmas Day because practise must be the priority, whereas a great champion like decathlete Daley Thompson used to train twice on Christmas day because winning was his priority.

Often, we hear a person hasn't got the time to go to the gym, but somehow, they find the time to go shopping or go to the pub. However, when a loved one goes into hospital, we find the time to visit them because it's the priority.

We need to make our progression a priority because if we're not progressing, we're going backwards.

Of course, we need to enjoy our time, but we can't throw those minutes away because each one is a gift.

Imagine being old and frail and looking back at your life with regret, knowing we could've and should've done more.

But who says you *will* be old and frail?

What if this is your last week alive?

EDUCATION

When I was at school, if you'd have told me one day I would write a book that involved a section on *education*, I would've wondered which planet you came from.

From my first day at school as a young child, I felt uncomfortable in the classroom, but as the years progressed the feeling of discomfort became more of a mental struggle and it certainly wasn't a happy experience for me.

You may be slightly puzzled if we went to school together, as I'm sure you won't recall me having any obvious issues. That's because covering my tracks was all part of the struggle.

To everybody else I probably appeared very average at school — I wasn't exceptionally popular or unpopular, I was fairly quiet most of the time, but not so quiet I brought attention to myself. I wasn't big, but I wasn't the smallest either, and the fact I appeared in the local newspaper for judo most weeks, probably prevented me from being bullied. Academically I wasn't the brightest, but I kept my head down and tried my best, so I wasn't ever singled out in that area necessarily either.

So, what was the problem? I fitted in perfectly.

As I've mentioned, I felt slightly uncomfortable from day one, but at the time I wasn't sure why. The other kids seemed to always know what they were meant to be doing, while I tended to look around in an attempt to catch up. There were many occasions when this used to happen as I recall, but it was most obvious when it came to reading. I think it hit home the most in my middle school years when we began reading books as a class and were expected to take turns reading out loud to the group. I would stutter and stumble my way through, and I would become more and more embarrassed with every mistake, made worse by sniggering that seemed to come from every direction. The only thing that used to deflect the attention from me slightly was the fact the boy who sat next to me was even worse than I was and used to get special help for his English. However, the humiliation I felt when it was my turn to read has probably affected me to this day, and it wasn't until well into adulthood I was able to see it in a positive light.

I think I was about eleven or twelve back then, but from then on, I would avoid those situations like the plague, and I would literally do anything to avoid reading out loud. During those type of lessons, I would nip off to the toilet just before my turn, or I would explain that I urgently needed to see another teacher about some work, or I would fake sickness. I think once or twice I pretended to be too ill to go to school at all and once, I recall developing a mystery eye problem which prevented me from seeing the pages properly.

The lengths I went to are laughable now, but it did make my school years extremely stressful. It wasn't just nerves getting the better of me as I'm still a terrible reader to this day, even in my head. I've never officially been diagnosed with having dyslexia, although when I answered a questionnaire online some years ago, it quite clearly suggested that was the case.

I used to avoid reading anything at school, so I wondered whether my lack of ability was simply due to a lack of practise. However, my mother-in-law got me into reading from my late teens onward and I've read hundreds of books on all types of subjects since then and today I can't get enough of them.

My academic ability, or lack of it, was almost certainly masked by the fact I was a high-level judo competitor, which allowed me to use that as the excuse for never excelling in school. If I struggled with home-work, I would use the excuse that I'd been training in the evening or at the weekend (which *was* true most of the time), but I pretended that was the reason for my work being slightly substandard, not the fact I'd tried my best, but it clearly still wasn't good enough. I was pulled up on it a couple of times by teachers, but I used to say I was going to be doing judo for a living and it was my priority. Each time I was told I couldn't make a career out of martial arts (wrong!) and that I needed to perhaps take more care with my homework, but it was never pursued any further.

Another reason I may have been able to remain under the radar is the fact my work was always beauti-fully presented and every single report I ever got would say exactly the same thing, *'Dominic is extremely neat, although he definitely needs to speed up.'*

So, in a nutshell, I hated school and I remember the relief I felt when I left through those gates for the last time like it was yesterday. Like most kids, I was always told, "Make the most of these years, because they'll be the best years of your life". I knew for certain that it didn't apply to me. As far as I was concerned the best years of my life were still to come, and I was dead right.

I never went on to college or university and began judo training full time. As far as I was concerned, my education was over. Like so many others, I believed education was just something we received at school and once we'd left, we were as clever as we were ever going to get.

I obviously knew I could collect more information from books if I went to the library, but why would I do that when I found books boring and I had no exams to study for?

It wasn't until I went on holiday to the South of France with Claire's family that my life changed to some extent. Towards the end of the holiday, we were sat on the beach and I'd become slightly bored with sunbathing, building sandcastles and playing bat 'n' ball. My mother-in-law (or my girlfriend's mum as she was back then) found a book her Dad had previously read and told me to give it a try. I'm sure I turned my nose up, but with nothing better to do, I reluctantly decided to give it a go. It was a war story and was the first time a fiction book had ever captured my interest.

I was familiar with the author, Simon Weston, who I knew had been badly burned during the Falklands

War in 1982, but the book wasn't about his experiences, instead, it was about the SAS. Realising I'd enjoyed the book, my mother-in-law produced another SAS book that her Dad had enjoyed, *'Bravo Two Zero'* by Andy McNab.

Like most people, I'd seen the footage of the SAS abseiling down the outside of the Iranian Embassy in 1980, but my knowledge in terms of what they did was extremely limited. I assumed they were called in when people needed saving from hostage situations, a bit like a SWAT team, but I was unaware they were elite special forces and took part in conflicts all over the world.

On the journey back from our holiday I was glued solidly to *'Bravo Two Zero'*. Being unable to put a book down was a new experience for me, and I read it cover to cover. The soldier's attitude to survive and win at all costs, was a massive inspiration to me and helped with my mentality immensely.

I went on to read many books about the SAS, but my new enthusiasm for reading led me to read books on many subjects I never expected to enjoy, sparking an interest in all sorts of new areas. During my illness, my love of reading would make the hours of toilet time slightly more bearable.

YouTube was founded that same year, but it would still be a long time before I had any clue what it was and how it was used.

At school, I enjoyed PE, art, and lunchtimes, computer studies were well down my list of preferred subjects.

I never took the subject as a GCSE and foolishly decided I probably wouldn't ever need it again (this was 1992 remember, how did I know what was going to happen!)

Being one of those computer illiterate types, I was always last to get up to date with any of the latest technologies and YouTube was no different for me. Claire had got me into Facebook, and I recognised this was *a must* if I was going to run a business effectively. I would post on there occasionally and formed groups and pages for my business (with help of course) but gradually I was noticing far more videos appearing on my news feed that caught my interest. Many of them led me to YouTube and I enjoyed how it would feed me new videos of interest.

Since then, I've watched countless videos, but the one which possibly changed my thinking and ultimately my life, was an Arnold Schwarzenegger training montage complete with Arnie voice over. I'd enjoyed all the Arnie movies growing up, but this time he wasn't playing a character. Almost every clip showed him lifting weights and posing during bodybuilding competitions, but it wasn't really about bodybuilding as such. He talked about how he had become a success despite many challenges and the message was really about having self-belief, which was something he had a tremendous amount of. I'll come back to this later, but the point was, it led me to similar videos where successful people told their stories and I gradually began altering my thinking.

Arnie's video made a lot of sense to me and set the ball rolling on my YouTube journey. As I progressed from video to video, I began noticing a guy pop up whom I'd previously never heard of — Tony Robbins.

Unlike school, where I had a hard time relating to a particular subject, Tony Robbins' videos really resonated with me, and the more I watched, the more they made sense. I was learning so much each day and gradually it became clear to me *why* I was happy in many areas and *why* perhaps I was struggling more in others.

This was an education!

The penny had dropped at last, and I realised for the first time that education didn't stop the day I left school, it could continue with Tony's help and a million other fantastic teachers that could be found on the internet.

I know there are many good teachers working in schools, but it's difficult to teach when the salary is so low, the hours are long and those that are supposedly there to be taught really don't want to know. To call the likes of Tony Robbins *'a teacher'* is a massive understatement — he's a life strategist and one of the world's top thought leaders.

The crazy thing is, on the internet we can learn every day — for free!

Even crazier is that we can learn while: cleaning the bathroom, eating a meal, hanging out clothes, washing up pans, travelling, sitting on the toilet, or lying in bed. That's potentially hours of learning time per day. The subjects captured my interest and I found that for once the information was not only going in, but it was staying in as well.

My attitude towards education has shifted so dramatically in recent times that it's led to myself and Claire home educating our own children. We started in September 2018, but we were thinking about it for some time before we finally took the plunge. It works nicely for us, as I mainly work in the evenings and Claire is a part-time nurse, plus we believe we know our own children best and feel we have what it takes to help them through the next few years.

None of them were having any real problems at school, but they were all getting lost within their classes to some extent. Ryan is smart without a doubt but was not excelling to the extent where they decided he needed to be challenged, in which case he probably wasn't fulfilling his potential.

Josh was almost the opposite, whereby he was slightly below average in the classroom, but not to the extent where he needed extra help. Along with most children in this category he seemed to be drifting through school, he wasn't enjoying it, and his confidence academically was quite low. Obviously, I can completely relate to Joshua's situation, but like me, I believe he has the potential to excel in areas that may never be discovered in the classroom. Interestingly, since leaving school, he's discovered a talent for playing music and is a natural pianist and drummer.

Lucy was neither behind nor excelling, but her trips to school were becoming entirely focused on her friends and the distraction was beginning to affect her progress. We felt that as time went along this was only going to get worse, so it was probably right for all of them.

One common misconception about home education is that the children are isolated from other kids, leaving them unable to socialise. People assume that children only make friends at school, but we all make friends in many ways. As adults, we don't stop making friends just because we've left school. Fortunately, all our children attend several clubs and have kept in touch with a number of their school friends, as well as constantly getting invites to parties and sleepovers.

There are many misunderstandings when it comes to home education, and until I started to look into it, I would've thought exactly like most other people. Another common one is that home educated children miss out on qualifications. For a start that is untrue, because they can sit GCSEs if they wish, and we personally know home educated kids who have gained good GCSE grades. It's very flexible and it's up to the individual what they decide to take, if any. It would be natural to assume those with more or higher GCSE grades, A-levels, or degrees are far more likely to do better in life generally, but this isn't always true either. There are people with degrees working in McDonalds and conversely there are self-made billionaires without a qualification to their names. I'm not saying they're a complete waste of time, but they're not always a necessity.

There are many people who gain qualifications at school, college and university, which turn out to be completely useless. We spend a lot of time gaining qualifications at a time when most of us have no idea which direction we're heading. Guessing which ones we may need, and then spending a number of years studying the subject seems like the wrong way round to me. In my opinion, it makes far more sense to get qualified once we know what they may be contributing to and in the meantime, I believe it's far more beneficial to study in areas that will be essential regardless of which path we end up treading.

I believe it's wise to have a good knowledge of English, Maths, and Science, as well as maintaining a decent level of health and fitness, but more than anything, I think we need to understand how *we* function as people. It's common for children to learn how the body works, but it's very rare that we learn how the brain works, or more importantly, how we can get our brains to work for us. If we understand ourselves better, it's far more likely we'll be happier and more confident once we decide what our life's mission is.

Far too many people work hard to gain qualifications to secure a career which they believe will make them happy, only to find it's not what they expected. They sometimes remain trapped as they're reluctant to start from scratch, but even if they do change, similar feelings or problems often arise, and they continue to be unhappy. Usually, it's not the jobs that cause unhappiness but their inability to cope with the challenges, simply because they've never been given the tools to deal with them.

Let's not forget, we don't need education solely to get a job or follow a career. Relationships are another good example of where people remain stuck or fail to find happiness from several partnerships. I believe this is less to do with luck, and more an inability to understand what makes us and others tick, but this is never mentioned in schools, unlike a lot of useless knowledge that is commonly taught.

Home education isn't convenient for everyone that's for sure, so it's unrealistic to suggest everyone should go down that route, but I hope that over time, education authorities begin to realise the current system is extremely outdated.

The current education system was designed during the industrial age, at a time when it was important to produce factory workers. Large groups of children were expected to sit quietly in orderly lines, follow instructions, react to bells and were sometimes rewarded for doing as they were told. Most of these expectations remain today, but as we know, the world has changed immensely.

These days, we're very unlikely go far by simply following instructions. The people we value most are those who can think outside the box, be creative, communicate with others and become leaders or role models.

It's extremely difficult to develop those skills within the current school system where everyone, regardless of their ability or maturity, must follow exactly the same curriculum, at exactly the same time and in exactly the same way. This makes it almost impossible to explore individual passions and interests which may allow children to find where their special or unique talents lie, ultimately creating a much happier path.

Many successful people either failed or dropped out of the traditional school system, but fortunately, they were able to come through. Not everyone is so lucky, and we have to wonder how many talents go unrecognised within the current system.

I used to think I hated education, but it turned out I was simply uneducated.

I started this book by saying I wasn't an expert on happiness, but as time goes on, and the more I learn from books, the internet, talking to interesting people and experiencing the real world, the more of an expert I feel I'm becoming. With time and effort, we can become experts in anything we want, because getting an education has never been so easy.

WORK

The word **work** can mean so many things, although most of us think of work negatively — something laborious, something we must do to earn a living or even something to avoid. Ideally, work should be something we enjoy, but even if we're not enjoying a certain element of our work, the way we feel about it usually depends on what we believe it's contributing towards.

In 2002 while training in Japan, I witnessed the epitome of work (in fact seriously hard work). Keiji Suzuki (one of the Japanese team members) was injured and was unable to take part in the randori session (judo sparring). Instead of sitting on the side, he occupied a corner of the mat with his training partner and drilled a technique by attacking with it nine times followed by a throw on the tenth...*for three hours!*

If you've ever done judo, you may know that doing this type of exercise for five minutes isn't easy, but the incredible thing is, after lunch, he came back and repeated the whole thing *again!* Even more incredible was the fact he never once changed the technique. It was a simple throw, from a simple grip, done in a simple way, but repeated literally thousands of times.

There are those that practise until they get it right, and then there are people like Suzuki, who practise until they can't get it wrong!

Just for the record, Suzuki became Olympic Champion two years later, so the hard work paid off.

There's no question Suzuki's training was ridiculously hard work and it's difficult to imagine many people repeating the same thing over and over again for six hours, but when we think about it, how many of us repeat the same tasks at work for maybe eight, ten or twelve hours, day in, day out, for years in many cases.

Why?

Because it's routine, it's what we do, it's what we feel we *have to do* in a lot of cases.

There's little wonder that a lot of people are bored, frustrated and disillusioned with their work.

There's a good chance that within the six hours I saw Suzuki drilling his move, he may have felt a touch of boredom (he may even have been bored out of his skull), but what probably kept him going was the knowledge it was contributing towards his ultimate goal, just as Arnie knew each rep in the gym was putting him one step closer to becoming Mr. Universe, a Hollywood Icon and an influential politician.

Work and even hard work is not the problem. Work without a positive meaning attached to it is the type we struggle with, and if we believe a weekly or monthly wage is a positive meaning, then guess again.

For the majority, the daily grind of repetitive tasks will never produce an Olympic gold medal or legendary status. In fact, this continuous effort may go unappreciated and even unnoticed to a certain extent, and the common fact is, any progress is usually contributing to building someone else's dream.

If our work isn't making us happy or isn't building our dream, we have two options available — *change the meaning* or *change the job!*

If our work isn't making us happy or isn't building our dream, we have two options available — *change the meaning* or *change the job!*

Changing our job every five minutes isn't particularly convenient, and unless we leave one job on Friday and start the new one on Monday, it isn't the best way to feel financially secure. It may not be the best idea to remain stuck in a job that is sucking the life out of us, but it may be possible to ask ourselves, "How can I make my work more enjoyable?"

Two lorry drivers with identical jobs may experience them in completely different ways, where one is happy and the other isn't.

Driver one may feel stressed because they leave for work in the dark and return home in the dark. They may feel under pressure with increasing workloads, they miss their kids, miss out on quality time with their partners and get paid very little.

Driver two on the other hand, may feel a sense of pride knowing their role is an important one and understands how life is made a lot more difficult for those who fail to receive their delivery. They may see a long day at work as proof they are working hard to support their family but use the time in the cab wisely by listening to inspirational people on the radio or on podcasts. They feel lucky to have a job and although they spend a lot of time away from the family home, they understand this allows them to enjoy weekends or holidays even more.

You see, two identical jobs, but with very different experiences. The only difference between the two is what they are focused on. As Tony Robbins would say, "Where focus goes, energy flows".

Lorry driver one would likely argue it's easy to say that when you enjoy what you do for a living, but it's the same with all jobs. I know judo coaches who make more money than me but complain constantly and seem almost depressed.

When I was at school, most of the boys dreamed of becoming professional footballers (soccer players) and several the girls wanted to become famous singers. But how many times have we heard a player in an interview mention they're not enjoying their football, or don't feel appreciated by the club or the fans. Likewise, we've seen countless singers turn to drink or drugs in a battle against depression.

So, before we change jobs, understand it's the attitude that will bring happiness, not the work alone.

In my experience though, it's the ones who are the unhappiest that are the least likely to change jobs.

Why?

Because the lorry driver ones' of this world are those who tend to make themselves the victims. They feel as though life is against them, others have it easier than them, they make excuses for why they are where they are, blame others on a regular basis, and believe they are stuck in their unfulfilled world.

Despite being happier, the driver twos' of this world may still take inspiration from YouTube or books they read during their break. Although they appreciate their current life, they have the belief to challenge themselves with something even more meaningful, possibly including more time with family and friends.

If you're a young person just starting out, or a person who knows for certain the job you're currently in is not for you, this is my advice to you. Think about what you would do if you didn't need the money, something you would willingly do for free. That's what you should do, find a creative way to make money at it.

It may not make you a millionaire overnight, but if you're passionate about it, you're much more likely to do it well. If it's a product or service you strongly believe in, it'll be far easier to sell it to others. There are tons of good ideas on the internet on how to make money, there's no real excuse for getting stuck in a dead end nine to five anymore.

You may say, "but I've got a family to feed, I can't just jack in my job like that". But that's the beauty of the internet, it never closes. If you finish your job at five, what's stopping you from developing something within the other 16 hours you have available each day? If it's something you enjoy doing, it should be a pleasure anyway, and if enough time and effort goes into it, the nine to five can gradually be reduced or even left behind.

Sometimes internet businesses can do really well, but even if it only makes you enough to pay the bills, the prospect of more free time and no more *Monday feelings* is priceless.

You may feel you lack good ideas and may not feel particularly passionate about anything, but once you start to change your mindset, it's amazing how ideas just start coming to you. I really didn't see myself as a creative person, but since getting into this type of mindset, I have had countless ideas for things I could do, and if I wasn't so content doing what I'm doing already, I'm sure I would've tried some new ideas out (that's not to say I won't in the future possibly).

Podcasting is something that has become way more popular in recent times, and I regularly listen to the Joe Rogan podcast which I find very interesting, with Joe often talking to guests about MMA and all things positive. At present, he has 6.8 million subscribers, which may have something to do with him being a stand-up comedian, as well as a commentator for the UFC.

On one of his podcasts, I recall Joe talking about a couple of unknown guys who started a Harry Potter podcast and it is currently one of the most successful in the world. So, if you have an interest that is shared by many people globally, it's possible to do something similar maybe.

If you have children of a certain age, I'm sure you're familiar with certain YouTubers, who basically chat while sitting around playing computer games, and according to my kids, some of them live in big houses and drive cool cars.

If we're going to spend a large portion of our time working, we might as well enjoy it, and if we manage to generate a lot of money in the process, it's a bonus.

MONEY

If you ask the average person what would be required to improve their general happiness, the majority of them would almost certainly have *money* somewhere near the top of their list. Some may even rate it as number one, and in today's world, it's easy to see why they would think this way.

There are countless videos online about making money and often a person will explain how to achieve it while standing in front of their private jet or their fleet of supercars. I understand that gets attention and people are more likely to listen to them if they're surrounded by lavish material possessions. It's natural for people to want the same for themselves, but it's also natural to believe money solves all our problems, which is not the case at all.

Rich people often have as many problems as anybody else. There are many areas we should try to master in life, and money is just one of many. Money can buy a lot of things, but knowledge isn't usually one of them. It takes time and effort to acquire knowledge and if a person spends their whole life only concerned about making money, it's likely other areas are being neglected. However, very rich people generally tend to be smart people, they understand spending money on their own self-improvement is a good investment. That's why the Richard Bransons and Oprah Winfreys of this world, tend to be happy and fulfilled as well as being insanely rich.

Financial wealth doesn't automatically translate into happiness and fulfilment, and there are many examples of unhappy rich people. They may possess the know-how when it comes to making money, but if they lack the tools to cope with their position, they may experience stress and can suffer from depression, just the same as anybody else.

Having a lot of money comes with its own set of challenges, and you'd be mistaken if you thought money itself wasn't any longer a concern. They may not be worried about paying their monthly gas bill, but there are many things to think about, including future security for the family, business deals, investments, and even taxes. Usually, the larger the amount, the larger the concern, if things go badly, the result would be a bigger loss, which can mean even greater stress.

It's a myth that money automatically equals happiness and fulfilment, just as it's a myth those without it can never be truly happy. I'm living proof that an abundance of money isn't a requirement in order to be happy.

As far as writing this book is concerned, I consider my current financial situation as a huge advantage over many people who may give you advice on happiness and success. When someone is giving you advice surrounded by luxuries on board their private jet, it's difficult for the average person to relate to them. Even if they're self-made and come from humble beginnings, it's very easy for most of us to think, "Well it's easy for you to say now". I doubt many of them were shouting their helpful advice from the rooftops before they were financially rich.

This is where I'm different!

When an ordinary person like myself, tells you I'm genuinely happy and gives you advice on how to feel the same way, then it's not only achievable but 100% real as well.

I know it sounds as though I'm against *being,* or *becoming* financially rich, but this really isn't the case. I just understand that money is *not* happiness, it's simply a tool to help create it. I believe genuinely happy people who are already financially rich, probably understand most of what is written in this book already.

If I ever become financially rich in the future, I'm convinced I'll be every bit as happy as I am right now, or possibly even more so. It's said that money simply highlights the personality that existed before money was a factor. If you were generous before you had money, you'll be even more generous with it. If you were reckless before you had money, you'll be even more reckless with it. So obviously, if we're genuinely happy before we have money, we'll most likely be even happier with it.

I know a couple of people that were once struggling financially, who had convinced themselves they'd be far happier once they'd made some money. To cut a long story short, they both landed decent jobs and did make a lot more money. But guess what? They weren't happy. In fact, they were probably less happy than before and continued chasing the thing that was missing. Unfortunately, they hadn't realised that *the thing* that was missing was a *positive attitude*.

Many people complain about the rich, which is often the result of jealousy. The problem is, when they describe a rich person, they will sometimes use words such as *mean, greedy, deceitful, liar, cheat,* and even possibly, *criminal.* If we associate any of those words with rich people, why would we ever want to be rich ourselves? We may think we're different, but that association has already been planted in our heads and it's difficult to separate the two.

So why am I not financially rich? I'm not going to lie and pretend that I wouldn't want to be.

Being a nice person has always been extremely important to me, even when I was a small child. At some point when I was very young, I believe I made an incorrect assumption that it was impossible to be nice, and rich at the same time. I'm not certain why I believed that, but I'm sure this hard-wired thinking was partly the reason for my poor financial progression.

There's a part of the brain which stores our beliefs, rather like a library or a computer. We add data to it constantly throughout our lives, which we can use at any time, but it's believed that everything we store in there before the age of about eight becomes hard-wired, which means it's far more difficult to remove or alter.

The only way to deal with this is to develop new beliefs to counter the old ones. This can be done with consistent, positive thinking, focusing on the right things, having the ability to change meanings and framing events or situations differently whenever possible. We will look at focus and meaning later in the book, so don't worry if this all sounds rather vague.

The point I'm making is my hard-wired belief may have restricted my growth in this area. That's not an excuse, it's just an acknowledgement of the problem, and nowadays I've re-framed this *problem* and see it as a *challenge* instead.

The first thing I needed to do was to change my perspective about who I was. I've always considered myself to be extremely rich in many ways and I've always appreciated my health, love from my family and friends, my comfortable bed, running water and enough food in the kitchen cupboard. That's not to mention thousands of amazing things we have all around us that a lot of people take for granted.

This was why I was happy to start with, but despite this, I never considered I may already be financially rich too. It had never occurred to me, that if we live in the UK, the States, or in most of Europe, we were already ridiculously rich in comparison to the rest of the world, and by rich, I mean financially rich.

Comparing ourselves financially to most of the world should make us feel much better about our own situations, but unfortunately, we only ever tend to make comparisons in the wrong direction. We see others living in larger homes, driving newer cars and taking more expensive holidays, and we feel as though we're missing out.

A recent study revealed more people would prefer to earn £90,000 a year with friends that earn £80,000 a year than earn £100,000 a year with friends that earn £110,000 a year. That makes no sense to me at all but says an awful lot about modern society.

If we can't allow ourselves to be happy unless we have the most money, I'm afraid it'll be a never-ending struggle, as there will always be someone richer.

One of the richest people in the world (and nicest, so I've heard), is the American businessman, Warren Buffett. His best advice for becoming financially free is to *'get ahead of the game early'*. He read a book called *'One Thousand Ways To Make One Thousand Dollars'* when he was just seven years old, and he began making money from then on.

That's great advice, but if you're over forty like me and allowed yourself to get behind financially, it's not particularly helpful.

What I have done, is pass this knowledge down to my children because I don't want them to make the same mistakes I made.

As a family, we teach them to appreciate everything they have and to realise the small things in life are in fact the big things. I was taught the same things growing up, but unlike *my* childhood, I think it's important to teach them the importance of money and to have a good relationship with it. By that, I mean I want them to look at money positively, to understand how it can be used to increase their own security and happiness, and how it can help others less fortunate than themselves.

My parents never gave my brother and me any pocket money growing up, which wasn't because they were tight. In fact, it was probably the opposite. If we ever needed anything, they would just buy it for us. We were never kids who asked for stuff all the time, but they never questioned it if we did ask, so it was all very respectful and it seemed like the perfect arrangement. The only problem with this was that it was all too easy, and we rarely needed to manage our own money. I say rarely because we were given money by our grandparents if we did well at judo competitions, so we did have something to put in our money boxes.

The problem was, I can never remember my money box ever becoming very full, so I must have spent it on meaningless rubbish, as I can't remember buying anything big or significant.

Adam on the other hand never spent a thing EVER! It was a bit of a joke at the time, but he saved everything he was given until his money box was full. He would bank it and start again, and very gradually it started to mount up.

He did a paper round, plus other summer jobs from about thirteen years old and started working properly soon after he left school, all the while keeping his spending to a minimum.

I on the other hand, never had time for a job because I was always training and competing. I did have a paper round for a couple of years, which I only did once a week, but again I wasn't doing a lot of saving because, in my eyes, I had nothing special to save up for.

My parents allowed me to train for judo full time once I'd left school and helped to fund my training and contributed towards my first car. I partly funded myself with small grants and landed a far bigger one (due to my level) from the National Lottery, which certainly took some pressure off. I wasn't after a free ride though, I wanted to pay it all back once my competitive career was over, or when I was more able to contribute. I kept a check on everything they paid for and gradually started to pay it back.

Believe me, my intentions were genuine, but the problem is, the older we become and the more responsibilities we have, the more money we have to find. Just when I'd almost paid the money back, something else would crop up and I'd have to borrow from them once again.

My parents had given me the best opportunity to reach my ultimate goal and I appreciated all the help I was given. But once I hit my early twenties I began to feel like a burden, so I needed a plan to make money while I continued training at the level I wanted.

I kept being told if I went into the military, they would allow me to train full time if I was good enough at my chosen sport. I knew guys who were doing just that who were not on my level at the time, so why not? This was prior to 9/11 so nobody really considered the possibility of going to war.

My plan was to become a *Physical Training Instructor* in the RAF, and I was invited by a friend's Dad to visit RAF Marham for the day, where I chatted to the instructors and even took a class of recruits for a warm-up. I'd already delivered many judo sessions at that point and it seemed like the job for me, especially because I was given great feedback from the instructors.

I went to the recruitment office where I took the initial aptitude test. I hadn't taken a test in years and my academic skills were not the sharpest, but all sorts of people join the military, so I wasn't too worried. But when I was called into the office and told my score was below the standard for a Physical Training Instructor, I was embarrassed, to say the least. I didn't fancy being a *steward* or a *chief,* so I decided to knock the idea on the head and mentioned my failed attempt to join the forces to as few people as possible.

One of my judo coaches at the time knew I was desperate for money and suggested I worked with him at a sign company. Another of my coaches ran the company, so I was given a few hours of work a day to help me out, and they were good about giving me time off for training and competitions. But as the company became busier, they were unable to accommodate my flexible hours. I wasn't willing to compromise my training for a few extra quid, so they asked me to leave.

At this point, I was the current British Champion, and I felt I needed to focus all of my efforts on the judo. But when I injured my knee badly and was out of competition for almost a year, it seemed like the right time to start my coaching business. So, that's what I did.

However, once I returned to competition, it was difficult, to put 100% into the business, and I was still struggling financially.

Becoming ill with ulcerative colitis set me back again, as I had to rely on incapacity benefit, and it seemed I was always playing catch up.

Later came the expense of having three children and buying a house, which set me back again, but despite remaining trapped on this financial treadmill, I'm gradually making headway. Don't get me wrong, I haven't got huge debts, but I'm nowhere near where I perhaps would've been had I made some slightly better decisions early on.

Now I realise my story in this respect isn't particularly interesting, but that's the point. It wasn't as though I made any terrible investments or took silly risks with my money. It was simply my carelessness in the early stages and my lack of urgency when it came to making and saving money, which I think was due to a lack of education both at home and at school. I'm not blaming anyone in particular, because my brother made better decisions with exactly the same education but looking back now, it seems so obvious and I wish I could go back and advise my younger self.

All of our children are far savvier with money than I ever was as a kid. We don't give them a set amount of pocket money each week, but instead, we give them the opportunity to earn it. The boys help me with different judo sessions and Lucy runs what she calls her *salon a couple of days a week. This involves her giving us massages, or doing mum's hair or make-up, which she's very good at. She's also started baking and selling cakes recently, and they seem to be quite popular. Ryan sells sweets and chewing gum at my judo clubs to make a bit extra and is always looking for ways to make money.*

Earning their own money instils the belief they're not just given something for nothing. One of the problems today is children are growing up with a sense of entitlement, which is no good for any of us.

We had bank accounts opened for each of the kids when they were babies, but we have also opened savings accounts, so they can start to build their savings straight away. We have taught them to monitor the amount they earn and transfer at least 50% into their savings accounts each month.

Ryan seems to have taken after my brother because he leaves around £50 in his bank account and transfers everything he earns into his savings each month. I know from experience that it gets much harder to save as we accumulate more payments, so getting ahead of the game while it's easy to do so is a wise decision.

Getting them into the habit of saving in this manner will continuously build their security for the future, without them ever feeling a sacrifice is being made. They'll always have money to spend if they want to use what's left, but like most things, spending becomes a habit the more we do it, so we try to guide them to make wise purchases if they ever go shopping. We rarely tell them any items are off-limits because it's important for them to make their own choices and occasionally make mistakes. For instance, if they buy some sweets and feel sick after scoffing the lot within ten minutes, or they buy a toy that gets played with for a day or two before it gathers dust on a shelf or gets shoved in a box never to be seen again, we may remind them of it before repeating the same mistake next time. Usually, they make the right decisions.

As adults, we rarely have anybody there to advise us on our decision making, but just like children, we can be tempted to make bad choices by purchasing silly items we simply don't need.

Probably the best and most simple piece of advice I've heard, that kids or adults can follow, came from the money-saving expert, Martin Lewis. It's simply three questions we should all ask ourselves before making any kind of purchase:

1. Do I want it?

2. Do I need it?

3. Can I afford it?

The rule is, if we answer **NO** to any of those questions, we don't make the purchase.

It sounds too simplistic to be effective, but it really works. Think about how many people use credit cards because they can't afford something. This has to be the silliest idea ever, because if you couldn't afford it in the first place, why will it become affordable with interest on top?

My brother has never used a credit card in his life, which is a wise decision. I *have* used credit cards, but even though I've never got into debt with them and always paid them off before the deadline, occasionally I have struggled because my bill was higher than I thought it would be. I know that sounds like a basic error, but it's a common mistake. It's too easy just to whip out the plastic whenever you need it, whereas handing over real cash seems a lot harder and at least makes us think before we buy.

Getting into credit card debt is like diving into quicksand. Once you're in, it's almost impossible to escape from without getting help. Getting ahead of the game from the start like Warren Buffet, or even my brother for that matter makes for a far more secure financial future and eliminates a lot of unnecessary stress.

A clever quote to remember is *"Act your wage"*.

Unfortunately, too many people want to spend more than they earn, but we don't need to be financial experts to know how that'll turn out.

American businessman and author, Robert Kiyosaki, used to look at this in a slightly different way. Instead of looking at how much money he had to spend and then deciding what he could afford, he would decide what he wanted to purchase first and then worked out afterwards how much more he would need to earn on top of his basic living expenses in order to have it. For instance, if he wanted to fly first class, he would work out the number of flights he would be taking that year and come up with a total amount needed to be earned before he could make it happen.

Kiyosaki's book *'Rich Dad, Poor Dad'* is the number one personal finance book of all time and has sold tens of millions of copies worldwide.

It's less about how to earn or invest money and more about the psychology surrounding money, which ultimately determines how much you can potentially earn or invest later on.

Kiyosaki's family were not exactly poor when he was growing up, but his family had what he described as a *'poor mentality'*, which was very much like my own family.

His father (who is his poor dad) was a smart man with a PhD, who was the head of education at his school. But when Kiyosaki was nine years old, he asked his father why they were never taught how to make money in the real world. His father replied that his job was not to teach them how to make money but to find a job. When Kiyosaki pointed out that a job was simply to make money, which was the only bit that interested him (not the job), his father seemed confused. When Kiyosaki asked his father why they never learned anything about money, he replied, *"Because the Government won't allow the subject to be taught"*. To a nine-year-old, that seemed silly, but his father had to agree. So, his father suggested that Kiyosaki spoke to his best friend's father, who was an entrepreneur and extremely wealthy.

His friend's father (his rich dad) agreed to teach Kiyosaki all about making money after lots of persuasions and took him under his wing before allowing him to work within his companies. The only condition was that he would never pay Kiyosaki a cent for his services. His reason was that if he started to pay him, he would begin thinking like an employee, and he felt that if he remained hungry, he would be far more likely to think for himself and create his own path, which was basically what happened. In other words, his rich dad taught him a job should only be to learn and acquire the necessary skills before forming a business, while his poor dad saw a job as a source of income for life.

Kiyosaki found the main difference between his rich dad and his poor dad was their mentality.

His poor dad would often use phrases like: *"Money doesn't grow on trees"*, *"I can't afford that"* or *"I'm not made of money"*.

His rich dad would hear this type of talk and describe it as an escape, implying they were simply avoiding acting. This is rather like someone who knows they're overweight but insists they're far too busy to join the gym.

His rich dad never wanted to be a victim of the outside world, like those with a poor mentality and educated himself, so he could create his own financial circumstances. He believed anyone could develop a rich mentality, regardless of the family they were born into.

I'm still in the process of developing my rich mentality (in financial terms), so if you're expecting some life-changing financial advice, I'm afraid you'll have to find it elsewhere. If you go to a martial arts class you'd expect to be taught by a black belt, not a beginner wearing a white belt.

I *could* just write down a few rules or ideas I've stolen from Google or YouTube, but I'd much rather be a real teacher than a fake one. Who knows, I may write a book on personal finance in the future, but I'm not going to pretend I'm ready for that yet. It doesn't make sense to listen to a motivational speaker with depression (they do exist), attend a slimming class run by a fat person (we may even know them), or take martial arts advice from an instructor who insists on only ever demonstrating moves in slow motion (there are hundreds of those and strangely they're often the most expensive).

I see money more positively nowadays and I'm sure it's something that'll start to come my way more often. I want more of it, but I can say 100% it'll never be top of my list. While we are in good health and have our family around us, we often take them for granted and money can seem so important. But if those things were suddenly lost, it would be surprising how little money would mean to us at that point.

For instance, if we won the lottery and then had an accident in our brand-new Ferrari, leaving us unable to move and in a wheelchair for life, how badly would we wish we'd lost the winning ticket?

So, is money important?

Yes.

Can money make us happy?

Yes.

But understand it isn't everything, and if you fail to understand the lessons inside this book, I'm afraid it'll mean nothing.

DREAMS, GOALS AND SUCCESS

Dreaming is the most natural thing in the world, and as children especially, many of us have hopes of one day becoming astronauts, fighter pilots, singers, dancers, racing drivers, or zookeepers (you get the idea).

However, it's uncommon for people to follow the dream they once had as a child, or even as an adult because they feel it's either unattainable, too much hard work, or they have no idea how to even start the journey. This usually results in them just making do with whatever comes up, which they believe is more realistic and achievable.

My dream, as you already know, was to become the Olympic Champion, and although I did take steps to try to make my dream a reality, I was clueless in terms of goal setting. I did want it, and I did work hard — *very hard* — but the problem with *my* dream was there was only going to be *one* Olympic Champion per weight category every four years, and as you know, there are thousands, maybe even millions of people all over the world, wanting the same thing.

There are many elements that make up a special athlete who wins the Olympic Games, so even if I had worked just as hard as them and had the same skill level, there may still be pieces of the jigsaw missing, and my inability to set goals successfully was definitely one of them.

My so called goal setting was along the lines of; *I want to win certain competitions,* or, *I want to improve my fitness,* or even, *this year I'm going to work really hard in every session,* but there's so much more to it than that. I clearly had no idea what I was doing, and I'm convinced that if I knew then what I know now, I'm sure I would've been more successful.

Let's not forget I still achieved a fair amount as a judo competitor, but my dream was always going to be more difficult to reach than someone wishing to become a paramedic or a train driver for example. I'm not suggesting those people have an easy route, but there are definitely more paramedics and train drivers in the world than Olympic Champions.

However, it doesn't matter how big or small your dream is, knowing how to goal set correctly is going to help tremendously.

So why would you take my advice — a guy who has never achieved his main goal? Surely it makes more sense to listen to people who *were* successful and who *did* achieve their goals. Well, you're right! That's exactly what I did, and after a while you notice the same patterns appearing if you listen to enough of them.

When I got into reading, I would enjoy autobiographies, which are written most of the time by successful people. I would mainly read about sportspeople, but I'd sometimes read about soldiers, actors, comedians or well-known celebrities, but because I was a slow reader and the fact I'd read fiction books in between, these patterns were never obvious to me and I saw them all as unique individuals.

YouTube was the game changer for me from the moment I saw Arnold Schwarzenegger's training video, which I mentioned I would come back to earlier. The original video I watched was three minutes and fifteen seconds long and was extremely motivational, but despite him mentioning several of his key rules in that video, they weren't completely spelt out, which was obviously what someone like me needed. So, it was fortunate the next video fed to me was *'Arnold's Six Rules of Success'*. This was a slightly longer video of Arnie giving a speech about his life where he explained how he had followed his six rules, which made him successful in several careers.

These were:

1. Trust Yourself

2. Break Some Rules

3. Ignore the Naysayers

4. Don't Be Afraid to Fail

5. Work Like Hell

6. Give Something Back

These rules are fairly self-explanatory but you should maybe take a few minutes just to watch it on YouTube because for the first time, a path to success seemed more like a strategy and made perfect sense to me.

As I mentioned earlier, I quickly became familiar with a guy called Tony Robbins, who again seemed extremely clear that the path to success and general happiness was simply a strategy and less about motivation. I watched video after video, day after day and I couldn't get enough of them. It was like a light bulb being switched on in my head and although I'd always considered myself to be a happy person, it opened my eyes as to exactly why that was.

I'd failed to accomplish my ultimate goal, but it became obvious *why* I'd failed and for the first time, I was able to let go of this *bullshit story* that it was due to bad luck, coming in the shape of an injured knee and a bowel condition. Of course, these were factors, but I knew in my heart of hearts if they'd never occurred, I would still have come unstuck due to my lack of self-belief.

I'd always been afraid of failing and if there were things I was poor at, uncomfortable doing, or occasionally frightened of, I would avoid them, just as I'd done with reading out loud at school.

Strangely that realisation was a positive experience for me. I started to feel a lot clearer going forward and ready to fail as often as it took. I also realised that failure and people's hardest times are often the springboard to better times, so again, I almost welcome tough times because I now understand that growth often follows.

I'll probably never again have a goal as big, or as difficult to accomplish as becoming an Olympic Champion, but whenever I do have goals for, my relationship, my business, or generally in my personal life, I feel so much more confident to attack them and worry less about the outcome. The old me wouldn't have had enough confidence writing a book or to go against the grain by taking my children out of school.

If we want to accomplish our goals, there are certain rules that are important to follow. You may have heard a lot of them before because again, it's just a strategy and it isn't rocket science. However, if you *have* heard a number of these rules before but you haven't accomplished your goals yet, I wouldn't mind betting that you haven't applied them correctly. If we stick to the rules there's a very good chance we're going to be successful, in fact, it's almost a certainty.

If we take a character like Donald Trump for example, despite how any of us feel about him, we have to admire the way he always gets what he wants, and it was no surprise to me that he managed to become the American President, as I'm certain he would be following most, if not all the rules that will follow.

1. Know what you want
This is the first, and possibly most important rule when it comes to goal setting. Quite simply, if we have no clue where we're headed, it's almost impossible to reach the target.

Author and motivational speaker, Simon Sinek, explains this in a way that illustrates the point perfectly. He uses the example of a person being asked to walk in a straight line from one corner of a room to another. If at some point a chair is placed in front of the person, they would simply go around it and continue their journey towards the opposite corner. Despite the instruction to walk in a straight line, the person would automatically decide to adjust the plan in order to overcome the obstacle because they know where the destination is, which in this case is more important than the route. On the other hand, if the instruction was to simply walk in any direction in a straight line with no particular destination, and again a chair was placed in front of them, it's extremely likely the person would come to a grinding halt, or they may change direction and head off somewhere else entirely.

If we know *what* we want, and we remain focused on the destination or the result, any problems or obstacles will be overcome as we adjust the strategy.

2. Know why you want it

It's all very well knowing what we want, but it's important to be clear *why* we want something too. The reason we pursue goals in the first place is to feel good once we accomplish them, so we need to decide carefully whether those feelings will be worth the sacrifice.

For example, if we work hard for several years in order to become a doctor, then it's more than worth it if we love helping people, we enjoy the uncertainty and excitement that each day brings, and we feel a sense of significance and purpose for our lives. However, if we only wish to become a doctor to satisfy our parents, impress our friends, and make a decent amount of money, it's probably not the path we should be taking, as we are never going to truly feel fulfilled as a result.

If we know *what* we want, and we remain focused on the destination or the result, any problems or obstacles will be overcome as we adjust the strategy.

3. Know when you want it

Rightly or wrongly, a lady who decides she wants to lose weight for her wedding day is generally far more successful than the average person trying to slim down, because she has a clear plan of *what* she wants, *why* she wants it, and *when* exactly she wants it by. Setting a date or deadline for our goals are good for keeping us focused and on track.

4. Be specific

Having complete clarity with our goals is so important. Often people's goals are far too general, meaning even in the unlikely event of them accomplishing them, they'll usually remain miles away from the result they were after. Typically, these goals may be to lose weight, to have more money, or to start a business. They may be quite common goals, but we usually get what we ask for, meaning that if the person attempting to lose weight drops a pound, the person wanting more money is given a pound, or the new business owner cannot make a pound, they have each accomplished the goal, albeit nowhere near close to the result they were hoping for.

Add specific details to your goals, and they are far more likely to be accomplished.

5. Write it down

Studies have shown those who write their goals down have a much greater chance of achieving them than those who don't.

Being specific and writing them in the present tense improves our chances, especially when we leave them in places we'll see them often, like the bathroom mirror, the fridge door, or above our computer screens.

6. Visualise

It's far easier to be specific about your goals if you have a clear vision of the result in your head before it happens. Successful athletes, actors, performers and artists often use visualisation techniques in order to get the best out of themselves.

If I'm honest, it's something I used to really struggle with back in my competitive days, and although I knew of others who used to swear by it, I didn't consider it particularly important. Any time I did try it, it just didn't seem realistic and I would abandon it quickly.

These days, I appreciate the importance of it and I now realise my inability to visualise was simply down to a lack of practise.

Someone who is fantastic at visualising, is the Irish MMA star Conor McGregor, who is probably the best known, and undoubtedly the richest MMA fighter of all time. In just over three years, McGregor went from collecting his weekly unemployment cheque of 188 euros, to earning close to $100 million for his one-off boxing match against Floyd Mayweather. Many of his other fights also generated several million dollars during the same period, not to mention his sponsorship deals with various companies and the launch of his own brand of Irish whisky.

Conor has made no secret about being motivated by vast amounts of money and loves to buy fast cars and designer suits at every opportunity. He describes how he would clearly visualise himself driving a soft-top Bentley through Las Vegas, while in fact, he was driving his girlfriend's old car that would often breakdown. But he thought about it so often, he could clearly see it in his mind, as though it was already happening, and later he was indeed driving through Vegas in his soft-top Bentley.

You see, Conor didn't just say that he hoped to buy himself a nice car maybe one day in the future. He was clear and specific about the exact car it would be, where he'd drive it, and as far as he was concerned, getting it was just a matter of time, despite (in his words), *"not having a pot to piss in"* at that time.

Luckily, Conor was able to visualise more than just himself accumulating material things. He would talk about visualising himself giving to those who had helped him rise to the top, but most importantly, he could clearly and specifically see himself winning fights, which was the thing that would ultimately make all his dreams come true.

There is a great YouTube video titled, *'20 Times Conor McGregor Predicted the Future'*, which is a bunch of clips of him talking during interviews, or even before he became well known. He clearly describes things that have already played out in his head, which is then followed by real footage of the event happening, often very accurately and sometimes several years later.

Conor often talks about *creating the Law of Attraction*, but there are many successful people who also believe it works too. Many people are sceptical about the Law of Attraction, but it seems obvious to me that those people overlook a very important element — taking action.

7. Take action

Taking action is obviously the most important element of any plan, so why anyone believes it's possible to simply talk success into their lives without taking any form of action seems ludicrous to me. We can't hope to become a millionaire for example, if we can't drag ourselves away from the TV.

On more than one occasion I've been told by people I used to train with, that they could've gone to the Olympics for judo because they'd beaten me when we were kids. Unfortunately, they'd forgotten about the twenty years of hard graft in between which may have made a little difference.

It's quite common for people to have good ideas for inventions or new products and then fail to act, only to see the same invention or product appear a couple of years later. It's easy to be annoyed and feel as though our idea has been stolen, but it only counts if we take action to produce the goods.

8. Get momentum

Taking action is difficult, but the hardest step is always the first one. Most of the time, people don't even get started on their goals because the finish line seems too far away and the task as a whole just seems too overwhelming, meaning that the majority of people simply fail to start at all.

Whether your goal is to climb Everest or to give up smoking, there is always a starting point. If we've taken the first step into action, we've overcome the biggest hurdle, although don't expect the early stages to be easy. We may be motivated and enthusiastic at the beginning, but we need to be prepared for that to wear off and be replaced by doubt instead. This is often when we think, "what am I doing?", or "I don't think this is really me."

The first time we feel like quitting may be the first of many, but that is the most crucial time to continue. The decision to start and the decision to continue when it gets tough are the two best decisions we can ever make because those are the points when we gain momentum.

Momentum is extremely powerful and is often underrated. Some people may just quit repeatedly as soon as they experience any kind of discomfort, they never go far enough to gain momentum at all.

The first step gets us on the right road, but each time we push through doubt, pain, or problems, the person that emerges on the other side is a stronger one, who is more prepared to deal with **future challenges.**

You may well be reading this and are currently saying to yourself, *"Yeah but I'm weak, I never stick at anything and I always quit when the going gets tough".*

Make no mistake, that's not you. That's simply a belief you have about yourself right now, but momentum has the power to alter beliefs over time. If you stay on the right road long enough, you will develop into a person who welcomes challenges, because your new belief will be that you can conquer anything. Instead of, *"I'm weak"* or *"I'm a quitter"*, you'll be saying "Bring it on!"

9. Be prepared to fail

You may think being prepared to fail is a negative attitude, but it's actually the opposite. Many people fail to go after their goals and dreams because they're afraid of failing, so never even take the first step. If you hate the feeling of failure so much you'd prefer not to even try, then I've got news for you that you're probably not going to like,

You're already a failure!

You've failed to even try!

Being afraid to fail is okay, it doesn't make you a coward, it's completely normal. Remember, I used to avoid stuff all the time, but it didn't do me any good. Being afraid of something but doing it anyway is what makes us brave.

Mike Tyson's first trainer Cus D'Amato used to ask him, *"What's the difference between a hero and a coward?"* ...

... *"Nothing! It's what the hero does that make them a hero, and it's what the coward doesn't do that makes them a coward."*

So, you see, being afraid shouldn't stop us. Nobody likes failing, but the reason we prepare for it is that it's almost inevitable. If the most successful people on earth have failed repeatedly, and continue to do so at times, then it's likely we will too. Failing along the journey is how we learn and improve. From now on, never see failing as a negative thing. Each failure is a learning experience which makes us better and stronger, hence why the most successful people have failed more times than most **people have even tried.**

10. Make sacrifices

In order to accomplish anything worthwhile and fulfilling in this life, it's essential to make sacrifices on a consistent basis. This is often the reason why people either fail to accomplish their goals, or even fail to get started in the first place, as they're unwilling to give up the things that give them some form of pleasure. However, pleasure and happiness are two very different things. Anyone can have pleasure, even someone who's deeply depressed, but happiness only comes to those who work for it.

Power, money, food, drink, sex — they can bring us immense pleasure at times, but none of those things can bring true happiness, which is why happiness is far more valuable than pleasure.

Health, love, gratitude, security and progress are far more likely to bring us true happiness and fulfilment, but none of those can be bought easily or given without being earned first.

So, the next time we pick a cake over a piece of fruit, a duvet day over a trip to the gym, a piss up with the lads over quality time with our family, or an hour on Facebook over an hour working on our book, we need to stop and ask *"Are we choosing happiness or pleasure?"*

When we make sacrifices, we often believe we're losing something, but in fact, we're gaining something far more valuable. Once again, simply putting a different meaning to sacrifice makes it easier. From now on we need to realise, the things that make us comfortable will lead to discomfort in the long run, and the things that make us uncomfortable enable us to become comfortable — mentally, physically and emotionally.

11. Find a role model

Once you know exactly what your goal is, it's a good idea to find the best role model possible to help you along the way. Once upon a time, having the right parent, teacher, coach, mentor or friend, was often a matter of luck, and if the stars aligned correctly it was possible for great things to develop. These days, if we have an internet connection, we have access to most of the world's greatest role models at the touch of a few buttons, it's far easier to get good at almost anything. Find that person who has what you want and simply mimic everything about them that will help you achieve your goal. Just watching one video about them may not tell you exactly what you need to know, so you will need to dig deeper into their childhood/background, their journey, their strategies and hopefully learn from their failures too. Take inspiration from their story and take on board any ideas that will help you on your own journey.

I was fortunate to have good parents and inspirational coaches to help me become moderately successful and more importantly a decent human being. But the role models I stumbled across on the internet in recent years have literally transformed my thinking and ultimately my life. It's quite exciting to think that your most influential role models are out there just waiting to be discovered.

12. Be different

After advising you to mimic someone else, I realise this sounds like a complete contradiction, but please allow me to explain.

Mimicking *the best* in any field keeps us on the right track as far as our goals are concerned, but what I started to realise was, the most successful people would generally share similar stories regarding their climb to the top, despite in many cases having almost unique personalities. Once you start to look more closely at their lives, you'll notice familiar patterns time and time again.

Successful people are usually:

- Extremely hungry and driven
- Disciplined

- Face their fears
- Fail a lot
- Use their failures to improve
- Never give up
- Don't make excuses
- Are *different*

You may have all the above, but if you're competing against many others who are doing the same thing, it's going to be extremely difficult to stand out.

When someone is very successful it's almost inevitable that people will attempt to copy them in order to create the same success for themselves. Taking elements of your idol's character can definitely help, although trying to be a carbon copy is quite cringe-worthy, especially when it's very obvious.

Before Muhammad Ali, nobody would trash talk, dance around the ring, or perform a lightning shuffle during a fight. But for many years now we've had to endure boxers attempting to clumsily win a war of words and shuffle their feet like a dad-dancer.

Similarly, 100 metre sprinters all smile and do silly dances on the start line. They talk to themselves, they pretend to brush their hair, they tense their muscles and fire imaginary guns towards the crowd or at the TV cameras. Why....because Usain Bolt did it, and he was the best — it's as simple as that! Before Bolt everyone was dead serious as though they were about to have a fight, their eyes focused only on the finish line, blocking out everything else and preparing to explode at the sound of the gun.

The problem with mimicking someone so precisely, is that you'll only ever be a poor imitation and you'll never be able to exceed the original.

If you're selling yourself it's always best to just *be yourself* and you'll almost certainly come across more authentic. If you're selling a product, I feel the way to go is in the opposite direction to everyone else and that is how you'll stand out from the crowd. Too often people tend to follow the trend because they feel it's the popular choice, but in most cases, your competition is much greater and unless you are truly exceptional, you'll just blend in with the rest.

The Sony Walkman (for those old enough to remember it) was a prime example of going against the trend and beating the competition. Back in the late seventies audio equipment such as record players, hifi systems and radios grew steadily in size until the latest models were taking up half of most people's living rooms. Instead of trying to compete, Sony Walkman went the other way and created a portable cassette player in 1979, which many thought was the wrong choice. By the mid-80s it was huge (not in actual size), and it completely changed the way we listened to music.

When I was younger, I wanted to be just like the guys from the top judo clubs and on the British Squad. I copied how they trained, how they fought, and even started smacking my own face before fights because that's what I'd seen others do and I wanted the same results.

But what I've realised over the years is, in order to be the best, you must be different, so now when I coach my kids I encourage them to look for inspiration from others and figure out how to improve on it. Then, if anyone is going to be copying, it'll be others copying them instead.

The likes of Muhammad Ali and Michael Jackson may have appeared unique right? Well, what you may not have known is that Muhammad Ali copied his trash talk off a wrestler he had met back in 1961 called *Gorgeous George*. Michael Jackson, who astonished the entire world with *'The Moon Walk'*, was apparently taught that move by a dancer called *Geoffrey* (doesn't sound like a big star does he?) Rumour has it he showed Jackson the move known then as *The Backslide* but it was renamed once Jackson had performed it to a global audience.

You see, becoming successful is not just about hoping and praying, because as the saying goes:

"A goal without a plan is just a wish."

CHAPTER 5

GOOD PSYCHOLOGY

THE BRAIN

After receiving an E in my GCSE science exam (slightly embarrassing), I couldn't have imagined one day I would write a book that included a section about *'The Brain'*.

Okay, I'm no neurologist, but the kids and I have recently been studying the brain as part of their home learning. We've been using Google, YouTube and a couple of Claire's nursing books, *so don't worry, I've got this!*

The brain is the most important organ in the body and controls everything we do (see — I told you I'd be okay).

I'm only kidding!

To be honest, I have a good idea about the brain and the way it functions, not just by what I've picked up in recent weeks, but over many years as a competitor and as a coach. I understand psychology for high-level sport, but I've also run seminars in the past on self-defence, which require a fair amount of knowledge on the brain's responses to stress and fear and how to deal with it.

The brain is almost two million years old, but despite its evolution, its primal instincts remain intact, meaning that it's number one job is to survive and cares less about making us happy.

Once upon a time, our 'fight, flight or freeze' response was there to keep us safe against sabre-toothed tigers, but that's no longer needed. During a self-defence class,

I teach how to recognise the 'fight/flight/freeze' response regarding a physical confrontation, but similar feelings arise in many situations, such as when we're about to speak publicly, attend a job interview, or even chat to someone we fancy.

Understanding these feelings are completely normal and using this knowledge to our advantage is extremely useful. Our instinct may be to avoid, run away, or hide, but often the correct decision is to override that response and be brave. Whilst tackling a sabre-toothed tiger isn't very likely to end well, the consequences of standing up to a bully, taking to the stage, going for that dream job, or asking someone out on a date, isn't usually too bad. Often, they can result in positive outcomes, which can improve our overall happiness.

The human brain is very much like a computer only many times more powerful. In addition to its logical processing, it's capable of complex development, learning, emotion, self-awareness, and creativity. But, despite each one of us overseeing our very own *supercomputer*, not one of us has access to a user's manual, which can make things complicated.

The brain is so impressive it can do any number of amazing things, often without any conscious thought. Something quite random that always fascinates me is our ability to estimate the weight of something without even realising. We use the exact amount of strength required to pick up a kettle for example, but the only time we ever notice it, is when our calculation is incorrect. If we pick up a kettle believing it to be full of water, it's only when our arm shoots up to shoulder height in a split-second, we realise it was in fact empty.

There are obviously certain abilities we are born with, but most of what we do automatically has been learnt and practised daily, including being either positive or negative.

Our daily habits or rituals are our equivalent of computer programming, and if a computer is programmed correctly it can be very useful. However, a computer that is constantly fed poor information and not corrected in time, can take a greater effort to fix. Luckily, if you've got the right person on the job, almost any computer can be improved and brought back to working order. In this case, I'd like to think that I *am* the right person for the job.

I could probably explain how the frontal lobe works, or how the cerebellum does this and that, but it may not be overly helpful. However, if you take on board some of the advice in the next couple of sections, I honestly believe it could change your life.

Some of us may have more knowledge than others when it comes to psychology, but I believe that every single one of us, including the greatest experts, are still completely in the dark about our brain's true capabilities.

FOCUS

Have you ever been on a car journey and forgotten parts of the route, even as the driver?

Although it seems crazy, it's a very common experience. For those of you that don't drive, I'm sure there have been occasions when a terrible headache has completely vanished while chatting, undergoing a task, or simply watching TV.

It's impossible for our conscious mind to focus on everything at the same time, so our brain automatically filters out anything that requires less of our focus. Fortunately, everything else gets taken care of by our subconscious mind, which is the human equivalent of autopilot. Think about it — there are all sorts of things we could notice right now; is there a clock ticking, or is traffic passing by outside? Can you smell food that was cooked earlier, or feel your clothes touching your skin? I'm sure you're now noticing at least one of these things as well as several others that are suddenly registering with your conscious mind.

If something is looked after by our subconscious mind it doesn't necessarily mean it's not important. I would say that swallowing and breathing are both important to us, but we can do both without needing to think on a conscious level. That's why experienced drivers can travel from A to B safely, without needing to think about every turn consciously.

Our brains can retain an enormous amount of information but far too much for our conscious minds to process, meaning we only ever notice what we choose to focus on. I'm sure we've all had the experience of buying a new car or an item of clothing and then strangely seeing them wherever we go. Why is that? Well, they were obviously there all along, but it's only once we have them that we notice them, creating the illusion of more suddenly appearing.

During the last World Cup, I found it very interesting listening to two sports reporters on the radio talking about the English fans. One of them was a Tottenham Hotspur supporter and the other supported Chelsea. The Tottenham fan was convinced he'd seen more English fans wearing white Tottenham shirts than any other team colours. The other reporter argued he'd only seen blue Chelsea shirts wherever he went. Even stranger was the fact neither could recall seeing anybody wearing the opposing team colours, and despite a bit of banter, they seemed quite genuine about their claims.

So what point am I making exactly?

1. We see whatever we focus on.

2. What we see is often completely different from someone else.

We've probably all experienced similar scenarios to the ones I've mentioned above, and it's because we usually see whatever we're looking for.

Tony Robbins demonstrates this perfectly during his seminars when he asks the audience to look around the room for thirty seconds and memorise everything that is *red*. He then gets everyone to close their eyes and while keeping them closed they're asked to think of everything that is *brown!* The sniggers from the audience suggest he's caught them out because of course, their full focus was on memorising everything that was red. He then gets them to open their eyes and unsurprisingly they are then able to see a lot more brown. He also suggests they may even see things that aren't there, for example, seeing something that's beige and calling it brown, just to feel more successful.

So, it's obvious that if we actively look for positivity in every single situation, that's all we'll ever see, whereas those people who are negative will always find something to complain about.

Are you a *glass half full* person, or have you spent your life with your *glass half empty*, always focusing on what's missing?

I believe I was a *half-empty* person growing up, despite always considering myself happy. About a year ago, I confirmed to myself this had definitely changed when someone handed me a tin of sweets and I joked that it was *'half full'*. It wasn't until a short while afterwards, I realised what I'd actually said.

Why has it changed and how did I become so positive?

It didn't happen overnight that's for sure, but by consciously trying to look for positivity in every situation, watching motivational videos, reading inspirational books and speaking to positive people, things gradually changed. Now all those things are like a hobby to me, and I no longer have to think about my behaviour, it's become second nature. I'm proof it works, but just like going to the gym, it has to be maintained.

We don't clean our teeth 2-3 times a day for a couple of months and think *"right that's all done"*. In order to keep them clean, we must continue to clean them every day for the rest of our lives. It may sound like a lot of work, but once it's part of our daily routine it becomes effortless and the results encourage us to continue.

Just remember, in life we get what we focus on, or as Tony Robbins says, *"Where focus goes, energy flows."*

MEANING

I mentioned earlier I grew up as a *glass half empty* person, but that was only the way I thought about myself due to a lack of confidence and insecurity regarding my intelligence. But the way I saw the world in general and the way I felt about people was very different, which is probably why I've always considered myself extremely happy. I understand I was lucky to have fantastic parents, as well as kind, considerate friends, but I also realise many people reading this book had a very different upbringing. If I'd have been dragged up by abusive or alcoholic parents on the wrong side of the tracks, my attitude would almost certainly have been different.

But make no mistake, a rough background doesn't necessarily condemn a person to a life of misery, any more than a privileged upbringing guarantees happiness. Some of the happiest people on earth were either abused as kids or grew up desperately poor, whereas most kids who are given everything from day one, possibly even love, struggle to appreciate the value of anything.

Don't get me wrong, I'm not suggesting everyone who has it hard as a kid, grows up to be a success story, nor do I believe every rich kid is heading for rehab. What I *am* saying is that the circumstances of one's life don't necessarily determine their path.

There are happy people and there are unhappy people, but the difference between the two has very little to do with their class or social status. The deciding factor depends entirely on the *meaning* they attach to their current circumstances — in other words — do they have a positive or negative perspective.

Nothing that happens in life has any meaning at all, other than the meanings we give, and those meanings are completely our choice. The meaning we give to something determines our feelings towards it, which can mean that two people with identical circumstances can feel completely different as a result of their perspective.

When people tell us to *"look on the bright side"*, it's actually solid advice, because that's all we're really doing here.

Finding a positive meaning is easier to do than talking or acting confidently because if we think a thought and realise we've attached a negative meaning to it, we can take as long as we require to think of a more positive meaning instead, which will almost certainly change our feelings towards the situation. If it takes a week to feel better about something then so be it, but as we get more used to finding a more positive meaning, it's likely that a week will become a day, or an hour, or ten minutes, until we can almost take a bad situation and flip it on its head immediately.

There are probably countless opportunities to practise this every day because it needn't be reserved for disastrous events. There are lots of mildly irritating situations that may occur regularly, such as dropping crockery, stubbing a toe, a nasty comment in your direction, the kids bickering, an unexpected bill to pay, or even just a rainy day.

One of the most common first world problems we often face is that dreaded moment our phone battery runs out, and we can't find a charger. For some people these days, you would think the world had ended, which causes them to be miserable. Those types of people are the ones who automatically attach negative meanings to everything, resulting in a miserable life. But it's simple with a bit of thought, to see a phone with no battery as an opportunity to start that book, or to get the car washed, or to go for a run, or even just have a chat. A good book can help us feel more relaxed, getting the car washed allows us to feel like we've done something productive, a run gives us a positive feeling of accomplishment and strangely, we feel more energised than before, and talking to people could help to either forget about the charger, find the changer, or maybe even borrow a charger.

It's no coincidence that if we attach positive meaning to a problem, things normally work out okay.

One of my favourite examples is the one about the two salesmen who open their curtains in the morning to find it pouring with rain. One salesman decides to go back to bed because he thinks the rain will keep people indoors. The other salesman smiles to himself and realises it's a great opportunity to sell some umbrellas and raincoats.

One of my students who was also a good friend was given 18 months to live towards the end of 2016. He died of a brain tumour in October 2018. We were all very shocked and extremely sad, because Wes was the nicest guy you could meet and had a wife and young family. As a healthy, clean living young man in his mid-thirties, it didn't really seem fair that his life was going to be cut short. However, when I saw Wes at a charity event the club had organised for him, I told him he was a lucky man. He looked slightly confused to begin with, but I told him this:

"Mate...very few people get to appreciate life like you will in the coming months. Savour every precious moment with your family. Most of us have everything, and we drift through life taking it all for granted. Enjoy your time and remember, it's not about how long you live, but the way you live it".

It's so difficult to know what people are really thinking, but at that moment I honestly got the impression he felt lucky, and all it took was a change of perspective. I'm sure there were several tough moments for them in the months that followed, but they experienced some special moments too. We all miss Wes, but his children appear to be coping extremely well and their mum is doing a brilliant job.

In life, there are only two guarantees — we're born, and we die. The bit in between is for us to try to work out for ourselves, but unfortunately, we don't all start at the same place. The country we're born into, our exact location in that country, our family background, the parents and friends we grow up with, all play a huge part in the person we become. This is obviously down to luck, or bad luck as the case may be. The great thing for almost all of us is that we're fortunate enough to be around at the time of the internet, meaning it's difficult not to stumble across some sort of positive influence at some point, even if you're not seeing it in your general life. This gives more people the chance than ever before to pull themselves out from the gutter and into a world of their choice *if* they're willing to work hard for it.

One such person is David Goggins who I stumbled across accidentally online. Goggins is now one of my biggest heroes and a massive inspiration to many people after writing his autobiography *'Can't Hurt Me'*.

Goggins was raised by what was seemingly a decent family, with decent parents, from a decent town in America. His father was a well-respected business-man, but behind closed doors, he was mentally and physically abusive towards his wife and children until his cruelty became so bad they finally plucked up the courage to leave and started up a new life in a much tougher area where Goggins was bullied and racially abused. He had ambitions of joining the Air Force, but because he was always forced to work night shifts for his father's business, he would either miss school or be too tired to concentrate, resulting in very limited education. This meant he was unable to pass the entry test initially, but with a lot of hard work he managed to make the grade eventually.

At that time, Goggins still carried a lot of insecurities regarding his past and despite excelling in many areas he struggled in others. As a black man, he was negatively buoyant and sunk like a submarine every time he entered the water (there's a reason why there are no top black swimmers), which made him very afraid of the water. This fear became so bad, he used a medical condition as an excuse to leave the Air Force without losing face.

Feeling like a bigger failure than ever, Goggins began eating junk food and gained an enormous amount of weight until he reached almost 300 pounds (136 kg/21 stone). At this point, he reached his lowest point and realised he needed to make a huge change — not just to his body, but to also to his mind.

After seeing a documentary about the US Navy Seals, he decided that was what he wanted to be and promptly quit his job spraying for cockroaches. These guys are as fit as Olympic athletes and are rock solid both physically and mentally, so as an obese man with a fear of water, it appeared to be an impossible goal.

This was almost confirmed during his first training session when he had to stop running after just a quarter of a mile. But he kept training and eating healthily, and the weight began to shift. Training got easier and each goal gave him momentum to chase another until he was ready for Navy Seal training.

By this stage, he'd calloused his mind to withstand any form of mental or physical challenge, but he was withdrawn due to stress fractures and contracting pneumonia. He hadn't voluntarily quit, so he was allowed to join the next batch of men attempting to conquer 'Hell Week'. He'd come a long way from that insecure, 300-pound wimp but had transformed himself too quickly for his body to cope with the gruelling punishment of Seal training. It took three attempts over the course of a year, but eventually, he fulfilled his ambition.

With his newfound belief in himself, Goggins relentlessly pushed his body to its limits. To raise money for some fallen comrades, he took on a challenge on three days' notice to complete a 100-mile race within 24 hours. Despite literally almost killing himself, he completed the race, but in doing so, he realised he could push himself further and harder than he had ever thought possible.

This led to a love of ultra-marathon running and after a lot more training Goggins was completing

100-mile races for fun. His longest ultra-marathon was an astounding distance of 205 miles which he covered in a staggering thirty-nine hours.

Just to prove he wasn't a one-trick pony, Goggins held a Guinness World Record for pull-ups in 24 hours, achieving 4030 repetitions in just 17 hours.

He lives his life continuously pushing himself to the limits, not because he wants to prove himself as an endurance athlete, but because he believes that most humans only tap into 40% of their capabilities. His only mission is to callous his mind to an extent where he can cope with anything that life can throw at him in the future. In his words, "I need to do something that sucks every single day".

So why am I telling you about David Goggins?

Goggins used to blame his upbringing as the reason he struggled to face up to the challenges of life, but at some point, he flipped the meaning for his life into a positive. All of a sudden, he realised that all the hardships he had been through growing up, was the perfect training ground for the person he later became.

Once we accept all the bad stuff and use it in our favour, we can achieve what once seemed impossible for us.

Goggins insists he's not special and believes anyone can do amazing things with a change of mindset.

SELF-AWARENESS, EMPATHY AND SOCIAL MEDIA

Back when I was trying to decide what needed to be included in this book, a section on self-awareness was fairly high on the list. I believe self-awareness is one of my strengths and feel my confidence in this area definitely contributes towards my own happiness.

However, when I finally got down to write this section of the book, I spent over an hour just looking at my blank laptop screen without writing a single word. I just couldn't work out why self-awareness was essential for making a person happy.

It's said that only a very small percentage of people are truly self-aware, and according to research, it's those people who are more fulfilled, have stronger relationships, are more creative, more competent and better communicators. A self-aware person is way less likely to lie, cheat and steal, they perform better at work, are more promotable and are more effective leaders.

You may think this answers the question, but how can we be sure a delusional person isn't truly happy too?

You see, this is the issue — if a person lacks self-awareness, how would they know? Maybe, they consider themselves to be self-aware, which has actually made me question myself in regard to my own self-awareness. I'd like to think that questioning my own self-awareness is an indication (hopefully) that I *am* in fact self-aware.

Which still begs the question: Is it essential to be self-aware in order to be happy?

I do believe it's possible to be successful without being self-aware. In fact, delusional people tend to be quite thick-skinned when it comes to criticism, meaning failure is less of an issue for them. Most of the time they see their failures in a better light than others and may even believe everybody else is wrong. Their persistence and belief in themselves (regardless of their true ability) is in fact, an enormous strength, highlighting the importance of self-belief.

I believe the difference between these two types of people is that a true self-aware person can see both their strengths *and* their weaknesses and are able to analyse themselves more accurately.

During his transformation, David Goggins regularly used what he called his *accountability mirror.* He created an alter ego named *Goggins,* who would talk out loud to David Goggins in the mirror. Goggins would be brutally honest with David, calling him *fat, lazy, insecure and afraid* etc, but he would also coach him on what needed to be done to change his life. Using Goggins to motivate himself, allowed David to believe it was someone else cracking the whip, which meant he had no choice but to do the work.

Despite being a *living legend*, David keeps Goggins around to be sure he never returns to his old ways. He has said many times that the discipline in his life is what helps him to remain truly happy.

But let's be clear — I'm not suggesting we need to become special forces soldiers, or Olympic athletes, to be truly self-aware. It requires brutal self-honesty, which is often difficult for many of us to do. Being honest about our weaknesses and tackling them head on is fantastic, albeit, simply accepting them is okay too. Putting ourselves down for the sake of it, however, isn't particularly helpful and only sends us on a negative path.

Becoming self-aware and having a true understanding of ourselves gives us our biggest advantage over those lacking in self-awareness, and that is a greater understanding of others too.

Social media is a platform where this can be demonstrated, and often highlights an individual's awareness of themselves and their empathy for others. It's usually easier to spot this in other people than it is in ourselves, but those who are good at both will usually receive more positive feedback than those who are clueless.

Even the best of us can make mistakes and say something we regret, but the beauty of sharing our thoughts and opinions on social media is that we have the chance to *think before we post*. Sadly, that's a luxury most people fail to take advantage of.

Those of a certain age will remember when people kept a personal diary, not to record dates and times, but to jot down all their deep dark thoughts, including their opinions on the world, the people they knew, who they loved and who they'd fallen out with. If these diaries were ever found and read by a friend, a parent, or a stranger, it would cause a great deal of embarrassment. Nowadays we seem to post about similar things, but strangely we get upset if it *isn't* read.

Our lack of consideration before posting and the subjects we post about can often lead to enormous problems, as I'm sure you're all aware. These interactions can create awkwardness, sadness and even anger, but ultimately over time, it can result in feelings of depression and even despair. It's been suggested many times that social media has been directly responsible for cases of suicide, which continues to become more common as more platforms appear.

I would say self-awareness, especially on social media, is more important than ever.

What we need to do, is ask ourselves how we would talk if we were up on a stage with hundreds or even thousands of people watching us?

Very few of us would talk exactly as we do on social media because we'd be too concerned about other people's perception of us. However, there's no real difference when we think about it and deleting something makes little difference if it's already been seen. Often people tell us they say exactly what they think on social media because they are *'real'* and don't wish to be fake, but actually it's more likely they're just lacking self-awareness.

Social media is often portrayed negatively, but when used correctly, it isn't just useful, it's a vehicle for spreading love and positivity.

I pride myself on the thought I give to my Facebook posts. I very rarely post my thoughts and use it mainly for work, but on the occasions that I do, or if I comment on other people's posts, they usually result in positive feedback from those I respect most.

Using social media wisely has nothing to do with the number of likes we get, or the number of followers we have. We need to listen, consider all opinions and think very carefully before posting, whether it be a statement, a reply, some advice, a disagreement, or even a joke. Many high-profile politicians, celebrities and sports stars have found themselves in trouble due to a comment that lacked thought.

Social media is often portrayed negatively, but when used correctly, it isn't just useful, it's a vehicle for spreading love and positivity. That doesn't mean we need to be posting motivational or inspiring quotes every five minutes, because a lot of the time it's meaningless and often comes from those who rarely follow the advice themselves.

The most positive thing we can do on social media is to talk to people the way we would like to be spoken to ourselves and only comment if it's something positive. If something requires constructive criticism and can't be avoided, think very carefully on how to approach it and really try to put yourself in their position first.

If someone posts something we don't agree with, just ignore it. They're allowed to have their own opinion however wrong it sounds to us. Telling them how stupid they are, is very unlikely to get them to change their opinion and only makes us appear confrontational, plus we become emotionally invested in something that didn't even require our attention. Remember we said earlier, *we get what we focus on,* so if it's negative, don't even need to go there.

In terms of posting ourselves, it's all very well me telling you to stop and think, but what should we be thinking about?

We should maybe ask ourselves the following questions:

- Is it important to anyone other than me?

- Does anyone else care?

- Am I making an interesting point or just complaining?

- Am I going to upset anyone?

- Would I get upset if someone else was to post something similar?

- Am I being funny or offensive?
(thinking from everyone's point of view)

- Is this appropriate for everyone to see?
(kids, parents, employers etc)

- Can I say exactly what I want to say, and it remains appropriate for everyone?

- Will I feel the same way after some time?
(ten minutes, a day, a week etc)

- Have I posted too many similar things?
- Have I posted it before? (or several times)
- Does posting it again help anyone?

As a person who runs a business, I understand the importance of posting things more than once, but I try not to be too overbearing with it. I'm sure I'll be promoting this book through social media, and I apologise in advance if I contradict myself on any one of the above. Having said that, I honestly believe everyone can benefit from the book's contents, so getting it out there is more than justified.

If I'm honest, people trying to sell their products or services on social media used to annoy me slightly, but now I see it differently. It doesn't matter whether they're trying to change the world for the better, or just trying to line their own pockets. Each one of them is trying to feed their family, so I'm a lot more forgiving towards it now (another example of changing the meaning).

Which brings us back to empathy.

Love and connection with others are vital elements required for true happiness. When we show sensitivity and understanding, both on social media and otherwise, it's a great way of building rapport with our fellow human beings and demonstrating we care.

Just knowing someone is listening, literally can, and has, saved lives. I'm sure we all have those negative friends who constantly complain about the world and everybody in it and expect us all to feel sorry for them when they post about their anxiety and depression. A large majority of those people are just attention seekers, to put it bluntly, but to be fair, it's not entirely their fault because they haven't found the path to become educated on the subject, which could enable them to overcome their issues.

However, there are those unfortunate ones who really do need help, possibly due to their circumstances or even a chemical imbalance and those are the ones who need our support. They don't always complain, in fact, they can often appear extremely happy. It's when those people appear desperate on social media, we need to act.

I have known a couple of people who have taken their own lives due to depression, and they were not the ones you would necessarily have expected. Robin Williams was a prime example of this; a person who was extremely talented and successful, financially wealthy and loved by people from all around the world. Unfortunately for him, the only person he couldn't make happy was himself.

Successful people can have seemingly everything, but sometimes they lack the mental tools to cope. This doesn't mean they're weak, because often they need to be mentally strong to succeed in the first place. They just simply lack the knowledge or help to find a solution during their darkest times.

It's a fact social media has saved people in the past and I have reached out privately to a few people who I felt needed some support. I'm not suggesting I've saved people's lives necessarily, but I'd like to think I helped them to turn a corner to a certain extent.

For no other reason, I believe this makes social media a worthwhile tool, and if that means we must endure some negativity from time to time then so be it. By improving our self-awareness and offering a little more empathy and support to our friends rather than attacking them, we can vastly enhance the positivity within our own world.

CONTENTMENT

Often people talk about happiness in terms of a destination they're searching for, and if we listen carefully, it's very common to hear the following:

"I'll be happy once...

- *...I've got the job"*

- *...I've left the job"*

- *...I've found my dream partner"*

- *...we're married"*

- *...we've divorced"*

- *...I've lost weight"*

- *...I've bought that car"*

- *...we have a child"*

The list goes on.

What we rarely consider, if ever, is that we may already be there.

Contentment is probably the most undervalued element of happiness but is often frowned upon to some extent, because if we're content with our lives, it can suggest a lack of ambition. We also celebrate those high achievers who confess to *never* being content.

I watched a documentary about the Manchester United manager, Sir Alex Ferguson, and his successful teams throughout the 1990s and 2000s. What stood out with Sir Alex and every player who was interviewed, was a complete discontent after winning a Premier League title, an FA Cup, or a Champions League final. Unbelievably, they'd be thinking about the next match before they'd barely left the dressing room. Of course, that type of mentality drove them forward to even more silverware, so it's difficult to criticise, but it didn't escape my attention just how many of them expressed their disappointment at not savouring each triumph a little more at the time.

In many ways, it's a trap we all fall into, where we constantly look at the future and fail to enjoy the here and now. We don't need to be high-level sports athletes to be able to relate to it. When we look forward to special occasions like Christmas, a holiday, or even just the weekends, we can overlook the beauty of the present.

Even once these occasions happen, we seem obsessed with displaying our joy to everybody else (largely on social media), so our most exciting experiences are captured through our phone's screen rather than fully enjoying the real thing.

Despite *knowing* it was the wrong thing to do, I fell into the same trap while fireworks exploded over the Cinderella Castle at Magic Kingdom in Florida. There I was, along with hundreds of others, holding the exact same position with my phone stretched above my head. This was an occasion we'd all been looking forward to for months, but instead of enjoying it, I was hot, dehydrated, squashed, my arms ached, and the action from the tiny box in front of my face was a total anti-climax as far as I was concerned. The kids loved it, so ultimately, I was happy, but a lesson was learnt.

What was the point of it? Was it so we could relive the experience later?

That's what we tell ourselves! The reality is that we're primarily trying to impress other people.

I think we've only re-watched the video once and that was only because we were transferring the footage from my phone to the computer. I never shared it on social media in the end either. There are countless videos of something similar on YouTube and I concluded that mine was probably no different to them. I realised those people wouldn't be bothered about watching my video when they already had their own, and anyone who hadn't been before would only feel bad because they hadn't experienced it for themselves.

So, who benefits?

Nobody!

A few months later, we attended a popular firework display in my local area and I consciously decided to simply enjoy the show, while everyone else took up the standard position. It was far more enjoyable than my Disney World experience, and laughably, I was able to enjoy four to five separate videos of the same display later that night on social media.

Modern society is far too concerned about comparing and *keeping up with the Jones'*. I've rarely felt the need to do this, either in general or from my perspective as a martial arts coach. I often get the feeling that other coaches in my position are fighting one another for members and have fallen out over it unnecessarily on several occasions. I've always been happy to allow my members to train at other clubs and learn from other coaches. I also try to take some inspiration from them too, rather than compete.

I once had a young girl attend my judo club who was visiting from a different club, but her family wanted to keep it a secret as they were concerned her regular coach wouldn't like it. I was happy with the arrangement but made it clear I would've been fine if the roles were reversed (some of my members currently practise at other clubs). After a short time, the other coach found out that she had been practising at my club and forced her to make a choice. I never applied any pressure whatsoever, but she ultimately chose us.

I think people can tell I'm very secure about my abilities and what I can offer them. I'm content with the situation and I'm happy for them to spread their wings if they wish to do so, which often creates more success in the long run anyway.

Too many of us
are chasing a
type of happiness
that doesn't even
exist, which is why
some people
will never be
truly happy.

_____

My brother is one of the most content people I know, and incidentally, he doesn't use any type of social media. Like me, he lives in an average house, drives an average car, but unlike me, he has what I would call *a normal job.* He was certainly intelligent enough to go to university and pursue a high paying career but chose not to — not because he lacks ambition, but because he's more than happy with his life as a family man. He's not impressed by material items and appreciates the small things most of us take for granted. But let's not forget (as we mentioned earlier), *the small things, are in fact, the big things.*

Too many of us are chasing a type of happiness that doesn't even exist, which is why some people will never be truly happy. We need to see what's in front of our noses and feel grateful for everything. My Brother's a fine example of this and I look up to him in my forties, just as I did when we were kids.

RELIGION AND SPIRITUALISM

It's fair to say I'm not a big fan of religion, not because I'm personally against it, but because historically it's been responsible for a great deal of conflict and discrimination. Over the years, countless numbers of people have been killed as a result of it, which has nothing to do with my opinion on the subject, it's purely and simply a fact.

Of course, there are several benefits surrounding religion if it's practised positively and I personally have some religious friends who are thoroughly decent people. I have no issue with people believing in a God, and why should I, because to me it's not about whether we're right or wrong, it's about living a good, happy life, regardless of our beliefs.

Some extremely wise and inspirational people, such as Tony Robbins, the Dalai Lama, Muhammad Ali (deceased), Will Smith, Gary Kasparov, Oprah Winfrey and Russell Brand (to name just a few) are/were all believers of various different Gods and religions, and I would consider each of them more intelligent than me.

However, I think we'd all agree, that Brian Cox, Stephen Hawking (deceased), Ricky Gervais, Stephen Fry, Richard Dawkins, Jodie Foster and Derren Brown, are/were all pretty smart too, and guess what...they are/were all atheists.

Interestingly, Derren Brown was once an evangelical Christian before becoming an atheist due to a lack of proof, while Russell Brand, on the other hand, was an atheist for most of his life, before he found religion whilst recovering from his sex and drug additions.

Arguably the cleverest person of all time was Albert Einstein, and he described himself as a *religious nonbeliever* or *agnostic.* If you're not familiar with that term, it basically means an individual, neither *believes* nor *disbelieves* in the existence of a God and concludes it to be unknown or unknowable.

So, what do I believe?

Well, as usual, I'm no expert on the subject, but I guess I'm currently in the Einstein camp. Let's be honest, it doesn't matter if we *are* in fact experts, or whether we're even smarter than Einstein. None of us can be certain of the truth, as there's no concrete proof either way.

I'm officially a Christian, but it's fair to say I've never really lived my life as one. My parents were never particularly religious, and it wasn't a subject we discussed at home, but Christening was far more common back when I was young.

At school, we were read bible stories from time to time, and we used to say our prayers in assembly, but to be honest, I was just going through the motions just the same as all the other kids. We may have visited the local church with school maybe once or twice a year, but it never really had any impact on me.

Don't get me wrong, at the time I *did* believe in God, because all the grown-ups in my life seemed to believe in *Him*, so why wouldn't I? (Just to clarify, that's not a sexist reference. It's just that a female God wasn't even a consideration back in the eighties).

Occasionally, I did pray for a competition win when I felt I needed some extra help, and as far as I remember, *He* did the business most of the time.

To be honest, other than the times I've mentioned growing up, God and religion never entered my head. I rarely felt as though something or someone was watching over me and if I did, it certainly didn't influence my behaviour. Luckily, I was a good kid, so as far as I was concerned, I didn't have a great deal to worry about and just assumed that if there *was* a heaven, I would likely be there one day. But that all seemed way in the future so who cared?

However, as young adults, we tend to think slightly more deeply into these matters, and it was only then that I started to adjust my opinions. Like a lot of people, I stopped buying into the idea that God was this old fella with a white beard, who sat in the clouds whilst keeping his eye on all of us simultaneously.

When we discover Father Christmas doesn't exist, we tend to look back and laugh at how gullible we once were to believe a man could travel around the entire planet in less than a day, delivering gifts to billions of people. So, I find it astonishing how many adults are willing to accept the Bible stories to be true. Isn't it reasonable to consider a person turning water into wine, walking on water, healing a blind person and rising from the dead after two days, to be just as far-fetched? That's before we mention stories about angels appearing in the sky, a person receiving a message from a burning bush, or The Red Sea parting in two to allow a large group of people to cross.

I'm not mocking the Bible, I just find it difficult, with what we know nowadays, to accept that the stories are credible. Put it this way — they are certainly not evidence that proves God exists.

It's likely due to those hard-wired beliefs that I mentioned earlier, that we form in early childhood, so in that sense it's understandable.

To be fair, it's completely understandable why they would've believed those types of stories 2000 or more years ago. They would simply listen to stories and there were no scientific theories to prove otherwise, it was really no different to our Father Christmas experience as a child. For us, it was simply that everyone we knew, including the people we trusted most, told us Father Christmas existed, and we had no reason to question it. That was until some kid at school spilt the beans and it made us think again. Back during those biblical times, nobody would dare to question the existence of God/The Gods, through fear of being struck down by lightning or some killer disease, plus they had no radio, TV or internet, with which to expand their knowledge.

I certainly haven't read the Bible cover to cover, but many experts have highlighted its inconsistencies and contradictions. It's extremely unlikely Matthew,

Mark, Luke and John were witnesses to much of what is written and it's debatable whether they were even real people. It's believed some stories were written as much as 100 years after certain events supposedly occurred, which makes it very difficult to accept them as truth.

For some reason, it's believed the Bible is somehow more credible due to its ancient origins, but surely this only makes it less likely to be true. Not only were the people who wrote it, far less educated than us, but they also had no scientific knowledge to support any of their beliefs.

But let's imagine all the stories in the Bible *were* witnessed by those who wrote them. How can we guarantee they hadn't vastly exaggerated their claims, or simply even made them up? Before dismissing the idea entirely, think about a time you were maybe out with a friend and an incident occurred that you both witnessed. Often their account of what happened is very different from yours, as it's not unusual for stories to be changed or slightly embellished. Over time, the story becomes less factual the more it's recited, especially when the tale is being passed on through word of mouth.

Another problem I have with the Bible as well as other holy books is the mention of practises such as slavery and stoning to name just a couple. Anybody who believes these have a place within a civilised society will probably need more than this book to help them out, unfortunately.

Of course, there are those who would strongly disagree with everything I've said. If you follow your holy book to the letter, you may believe I'm now destined for Hell. Maybe you're right, but I'll risk it.

The way I see it is that if I *am* wrong, there's a good chance I'll be forgiven and sent to Heaven anyway.

Why?

I always try my very best to be a good person, not because I believe there's a God checking up on me, but because I simply like being good in general. I'm by no means perfect, but I'm no less perfect than any believer in my opinion. Good is good and bad is bad. Why should the motive for our behaviour make any difference?

I realise that so far, I've sounded a lot more like an atheist than an agnostic, but I do think it's very closed-minded and even slightly arrogant to dismiss the likelihood of any type of higher force existing.

Most religious people describe their belief as nothing more than blind faith. A large percentage of them have no reason to believe, other than the fact someone else told them to, at some stage in their past. But when Russell Brand explains why he believes a higher power could likely exist; it makes perfect sense to me.

Russell says in his own unique way, *"anything that we're describing through science, we describe them through the prism of the five limited senses — our eyes can only see between infra-red light and ultra-violet light, there's light bouncing around everywhere — our ears can only hear a tiny decibel range, we can't hear the noise of a dog whistle, we can't hear any high-pitched frequency sounds. Isn't it likely then, there are other vibrations, frequencies, energies, consciousness, moving through the universe"?*

Again, it doesn't prove anything, but when put to us like that, it certainly sounds as though it could be possible.

But what does it matter? Why do we need an answer or confirmation that we're correct?

Throughout recorded history anywhere between eight and 12000 gods have been worshipped, so if you do believe in a specific god, what is the likelihood your god is the correct one?

To me, being a believer or non-believer is not the issue. Being genuinely happy and content with ourselves is what's important. If you feel your higher power guides you through life and you feel it necessary to worship in order to achieve happiness and contentment, that's good because it works for you.

Some people are spiritual without being religious and often use meditation to tune into alternative frequencies. Some people claim to be able to do it, and whether they can or not is of no interest to me, although once again, if it works for them, it's good.

Personally, I'm happy without being spiritual and I'm perfectly content not having all the answers. It's very unlikely these questions will ever be answered and even if they are, it's not likely to be any time soon.

DEATH

Religion divides many people because it provides so few concrete answers, and just as baffling, is the subject of death. Religion can be ignored if we have no interest in it, but death is a certainty for all of us, so it's something we all think about from time to time.

Happiness and death do not generally go hand in hand, but even happy people die eventually, so it's something we really must address. Death can make us desperately unhappy and is also one of the most common human fears, which can often prevent us from really living life to the full.

If I'm completely honest, death is one of my biggest fears, but luckily, I've found a way to attach a positive meaning to it, which helps me not only deal with it but almost welcome it. Of course, I don't want to die, but I tell myself that my fear of death is due to my love for life, which is a good thing. However, if I had the opportunity to live forever, I honestly wouldn't take it. I know that sounds like a strange thing for someone with a fear of death to say, but I believe we need the inevitability of death to be able to experience life's beauty to the full.

We tend to view death negatively, but we overlook its value. Often, we hear people say life is cruel because we see and experience illness and tragedy and loved ones can be taken from us indiscriminately. But as weird as it sounds, that's what helps us appreciate life while we have it and knowing that any moment might be our last is what makes it so special.

Death is a natural process, so why should we be afraid of it? It kind of makes it easier to know that every human being will experience it, as will every mammal, bird, fish, insect, and plant. That helps me to believe the experience won't be too bad, and if it is, then I'm guessing it'll be a temporary feeling that goes away. I'd like to think we won't feel a thing, just the same as when we fall asleep without knowing it. However, when we sleep there is still brain function, whereas with death the brain switches itself off completely, so I would assume there is even less consciousness or none whatsoever.

I really have no clue, which is no different to anybody else. In fact, the unknown is usually the thing that scares us the most, and with that in mind, it's worth recalling every experience we've ever had that frightened us prior to the event. I think you'd agree, almost 100% of the time, the fear we felt beforehand was far worse than the experience itself.

I think it's probably fair to say death is more difficult for the loved ones who are left behind, as they not only have to deal with the stresses beforehand but also the aftermath, which many of us can already relate to.

As a man in my early forties, I know I've been quite fortunate so far in terms of the people I've lost. But unless anything happens to me in the near future, I know that's definitely going to change, and although losing those closest to us is painful, I believe I'm as prepared to deal with it as I could be, so I no longer fear it in the same way I used to. I've come to realise that with the right attitude, we can cope with anything by looking for the positives and attaching a meaning that allows us to continue, knowing everything will be okay. If we can hold on to these beliefs during our darkest moments, we can develop a bulletproof mindset that can make our everyday struggles seem easy.

Studies have shown that accident victims are generally happier than lottery winners a year or two after their life-changing experience, which makes me think the same could be true for those who have lost a parent, a spouse, or even a child. With the correct mindset, I believe it's entirely possible to appreciate the tiny pleasures we miss when we're caught up in the rat race of life which is often so meaningless.

That's not suggesting for a second we shouldn't be sad regarding a loved one's death. In fact, it's quite the opposite. Sometimes, if we suppress those feelings and don't allow ourselves to grieve, I think it makes the recovery far more difficult and moving on becomes almost impossible. It doesn't mean we should cry non-stop for a week and then forget about them entirely, it's important to give ourselves time to come to terms with it instead of pretending everything is normal.

The grieving process is necessary and extremely natural. It may take days, weeks, months, or even years. Some people say it never stops, but regardless of how we feel, we can't allow it to stop us from moving forwards and living the rest of our own lives.

Of course, the death of a loved one is upsetting, but alongside birth, death is the only other guarantee, so we need to be prepared for it and accept it when it happens. Death doesn't discriminate, which bonds us with every other living thing on earth. If we're in a survival situation with a bunch of other people, it wouldn't matter whether they were male or female, good or evil, rich or poor, famous or unknown. In those moments, everyone becomes equal, because we all share the same emotions when dealing with death.

Former professional footballer, Rio Ferdinand, spent the best years of his career playing for Manchester United when they were one of the best teams in the world. Not long after his retirement he tragically lost his wife to cancer, leaving him to raise their children alone. He may well have been one of the most recognisable faces in the world of football, who earned more money in a month than most people would earn in a lifetime, but when tragedy struck, it counted for absolutely nothing.

To help him with his recovery, he made a documentary called 'Rio Ferdinand – Being Mum and Dad', which looked at how he had coped over the two years since his wife's passing. He explained how his career as a footballer had possibly made the process even more difficult because playing for a team like United meant he'd lived almost inside a type of bubble, where almost every responsibility was removed in order for them to concentrate solely on winning football matches. His wife had been on board with this also, so once he found himself in the position that he did, he was clueless about a lot of areas that would generally be easy for normal folk to manage. For instance, when one of his children became sick, he automatically contacted the Manchester United club doctor, who reminded him he no longer played for the team, and he had to register the children with a local surgery. He had no idea how to book flights or check into an airport, which was strange for someone who had flown countless times with the club. This had always been taken care of by the staff, and they had always been ushered through flight lounges and straight onto planes without any fuss.

For Rio, managing day-to-day life and looking after the children as expertly as his wife, while at the same time continuing a TV career as a football pundit, was unquestionably a tough challenge. It certainly kept him busy, but unfortunately, it prevented him from making time for himself, and he was unable to grieve as he perhaps should have.

The documentary allowed him to finally address it and face his demons. He spoke to groups of ordinary men who had also lost partners in tragic circumstances and it enabled him to communicate with those who understood. For once, he was not Rio Ferdinand the footballer, but just another poor guy who had lost his wife.

He also travelled to Ireland to speak with Darren Clarke, the golfer, who had also lost his wife to cancer almost ten years previously. Darren could see Rio was struggling and told him to be thankful for the time he'd had with his wife, rather than focus on what he'd lost, but assured him he *could*, and *would* be happy again in the future. It had happened to Darren, and he claimed to be as happy as he was before his wife passed away, which he once believed was impossible.

On the return flight from Ireland, Rio smiled genuinely for the first time in a long time. It was as though Darren had given him permission to be happy again.

He'd always found it difficult to show his emotions, but his breakthrough allowed him to open up with his children, and they began reminiscing about the happy memories. Previously, their brief and sporadic discussions had come from a sad place, which had discouraged them all from talking about it. But now they enjoyed it and the family came up with the idea of a memory jar, meaning they would all write about a happy time and pop the memory into the jar to remind them again another time.

As far as I'm aware, Rio Ferdinand has found happiness once again. During the documentary, he'd expressed his discomfort at even the thought of taking off his wedding ring. But several of the widowers he'd met insisted that removing their ring was an essential stepping stone required to move on. At that point, Rio could never imagine removing his ring and certainly didn't believe he could ever find another partner. However, Rio not only found someone else, but they are currently engaged, and the children are happy.

It's not something Claire and I have discussed a great deal, but she once told me that if anything ever happened to me, she could never be with anyone else. But that wouldn't be what I would want for her. I believe she could find someone else and find happiness again because I think we all need a special someone to share our lives with, and I would hate the thought of her ever being lonely.

I get that it's difficult for most people to understand, especially if you're happily married. I'm very happily married and know 100% that Claire and I will be together for life, but I've never bought into the whole *love at first sight* thing, or when people say they've *found the one*. What are the chances that you've found *the one* out of 7.7 billion people and how ludicrous is it that you would even live in the same country, let alone the same area or on the same street? What I'm trying to suggest is, we're all compatible with more than just one person and if we truly love our other half, surely, we'd want them to be happy if we were no longer around.

Not so long ago I heard an extremely moving story about a lady called Brenda Schmitz, who had died of ovarian cancer in 2011. Before her death, she had typed a letter to give to a close friend to keep until an unknown time in the future. Her instructions were to send the letter to a specific radio station, only when it was the right time. Eventually, it *was* the right time and the friend mailed the letter to the radio station, who then called David, the husband she had left behind, onto the show for a chat. They began by talking a bit about his wife and David struggled to keep his composure as he remembered how fantastic she had been as a wife and mother, and how strong she had remained leading up to her death. David, who was unaware the letter even existed, was stunned when they revealed the letter and read it to him aloud. The reason it was the right time, was because David had been raising their three boys, including a two-year-old called Max, but now he'd managed to find love again and had recently got engaged to remarry. It was Brenda's wish to send them all gifts through the station's Christmas Wish Program, among them a days' spa for her children's new mum.

I love this story because it confirmed to David how lucky he'd been to have his wife, but he was also free of any guilt he may have felt regarding his life with his new fiancée.

Falling in love with people is not always planned, especially after we've lost someone we expected to share the rest of our lives with, but it doesn't mean it's wrong.

Of course, I've never been in that position but can relate to it in a very small way. A few years ago, we bought a kitten, but I must admit initially I was dead against it. However, after much persuasion from Claire and the kids, I finally gave in, although I had every intention of keeping out of its way. I was convinced that a cat would be selfish, unfriendly, disloyal, would scratch the furniture and would constantly bring home unwanted gifts such as birds and mice. Not only that, but I recalled picking up cats as a child and hating the feel of them in my arms.

I wasn't happy about it, but I'd been outnumbered, so our new kitten, Bindi, came to live with us. I was even less happy when I realised on day one I'd be her sole carer, as Claire was out at work all day and the kids were at school. We were lumbered with one another and it's difficult to say who was the least comfortable, me or Bindi. She spent several hours in the carrier we'd brought her home in, as she was too shy to come out. But gradually she found the confidence to emerge briefly before retreating once again to the safety of the carrier. I was doing some paperwork, but I kept noticing her little head peeping around the corner and then disappearing again and I couldn't help but find her cute. I began talking to her to try to entice her into the room and very slowly she started to feel more at home. I got down on the floor and started to play with her and surprisingly, we started to bond. I picked her up and her fur was so soft and holding her felt very natural. She was still clearly on edge, but I felt we'd started to form some trust and when the others returned home, they couldn't believe it.

Years later we still have what I consider to be a special bond. She sleeps at the bottom of our bed, wakes us up in the morning, we *head bump* when I return home from work, and she often sits on me when I'm on the sofa.

Yes, she does scratch the furniture, and she occasionally does bring us a gift from outside, but I understand that's her instinct and it no longer bothers me.

So, if you were to ask me if it's possible to fall in love with another person after your spouse or partner has passed away, I would say yes. I know the cat analogy isn't quite the same, but I was determined to not even like Bindi, so it was very unexpected when I fell head over heels in love with her. She's no longer just a cat to me, or in fact just *our cat*. *I consider her part of our family and will find it difficult when she passes away.*

But as I've learnt over time, death for myself or others shouldn't be feared. Life continues no matter what, and we look at death as simply the end. If we make the most of our lives and make an impact on people, whether it be our kids, our family, our friends, or even the world, we can live on in some way.

I was once told to imagine my own death as part of a timeline. If we can see a time beyond that point and see it vividly, it doesn't seem as bad when we make our way back through time towards our death. For me, that helped. It made it far less final and today I have a far healthier relationship with death.

For many of us, death is the worst thing we can imagine, so if we can learn to use that to our advantage, what else is there to really worry about.

THE JOURNEY TOWARDS 'WORLD CLASS HAPPINESS'

After reading this book within a few days or weeks, it's probably difficult to tell it's actually taken me years to write. Some books can be written within a couple of months, but I guess I'm still that kid from school who *'does beautiful work but just needs to speed up.'*

I originally started thinking about writing it in 2015 after I'd finished my book about armbars. I really enjoyed the process but wanted to challenge myself by writing about something I wasn't necessarily known for.

It had been suggested in the past by a number of people, that my failings as a judo player may have been partly due to being a little too nice, and that element of nastiness may have been the ingredient that was lacking in that particular field.

But I enjoyed being nice because it made me happy and without realising it, being nice and being happy were more important to me than the thing I'd spent my whole life chasing.

After all those years, it suddenly occurred to me that being happy was the thing I was best at all along because I wouldn't sacrifice it for anything. I'd wanted so badly to be the best in the world at something and at that moment I realised I was possibly *world-class* at being happy.

Not everyone wants to be the best at judo, football, swimming or running. Not everyone wants to be a top scientist, mathematician, or surgeon. But answer this: Who on the planet doesn't want to be happy?

Being world-class at happiness was probably the best thing I could ever choose, and at that moment I knew I needed to write a book.

I was genuinely happier than anybody else I knew, and as I mentioned in the first chapter, there was literally nobody on the planet I would've swapped lives with and still wouldn't today.

But as I've mentioned many times throughout the book, I wasn't an expert, and I had to learn why I was so happy and why in many cases, other people weren't. This was probably why the book took so long to complete.

Looking back now, I realise that a lot of the answers were inside me already, because even before I consciously began studying the subject, I'd already learnt so much from my experiences as an athlete, as a coach and as a parent. I'd been given some great advice over the years by my family and friends, my coaches, psychologists, and even my competitors, not to mention information and ideas I'd learnt from countless autobiographies.

It's probably fair to say I've become almost obsessed with learning and understanding happiness, and since 2015 I've watched YouTube videos on the subject daily, as well as reading many books alongside writing my own.

I may have been at an advantage from the beginning because I was already extremely happy, and I was surrounded by happy people. But if you're not happy and you're in a dark place right now, you need to start surrounding yourself with happy and positive people. They say, *'we become like the five people we spent the most time with'*, which is why we need to choose the company we keep very carefully.

This may be difficult if you come from a rough area, or your family are not setting the best example. But this isn't an excuse, because people from all walks of life have become happy and fulfilled, and as an individual, it's up to you to take responsibility for your life and make the change.

It doesn't matter who you are, change is difficult and rarely happens overnight. In fact, change is probably the wrong word, because progression and momentum are far more accurate, as the transformation happens over time after we decide to commit to something and keep up the consistency.

Of course, it's going to be hard, as it is for every single one of us including me, but when we see the results it encourages us to continue on that path. When times get tough, that's not the time to give up. That's the time to be even more disciplined and consistent because that's when the changes will happen. We may not see the changes immediately, but they will happen.

If you're surrounded by a bunch of losers, get on YouTube and make the world's most inspirational people your new best friends. With time, their positivity *will* begin to rub off and you'll find happy and positive people in the *real world* will become more attracted to you and soon you'll create a new social *circle*.

The losers in your life will either reject you or become inspired by you, but either way, you'll be happy and equipped to face the world head on.

Remember, *'when you change the way you look at things, the things you look at change'*.

Another important thing to remember is that becoming the next Tony Robbins, isn't necessarily going to make *you* happy. You don't need to be a motivational speaker, write books, or feed millions around the world. You don't need to break endurance records or train like David Goggins. You don't need to be a winner like Usain Bolt. You don't need to be rich like Bill Gates. You don't need to care for the sick and the poor like Mother Teresa. You don't need to seek adventure like Bear Grylls, and you certainly don't need to be famous and successful like Arnold Schwarzenegger.

You don't even need to be like me, because it's all about what makes *you* happy and everyone can achieve world-class happiness if they have the tools.

I started this book by saying I wasn't an expert, but I love the fact it's taken me so long to complete because I can finish it by saying this,

I now believe I *am* an expert, but in terms of being a world-class expert, I really don't know for sure. What I do know is that the judo players who practise every day with passion, often become world-class judo players. They can do it with their eyes shut, and if necessary, they could use it effectively without thinking if they were ever suddenly attacked in the street.

Life can suddenly attack us too, but with the tools we now have, and with continuous practise, we can easily and effectively defend ourselves, by using our WORLD-CLASS HAPPINESS.

ACKNOWLEDGEMENTS

If I took the time to thank every single person who has contributed towards my happiness, I'd probably be here a long time.

I've been extremely lucky to have met so many great people throughout my journey, and I want to say a big thank you to everyone who has added something to it. Some of you will realise you've played a big part in my development, but many of you will have no idea I'm talking to you too. Believe me, we find sparks of inspiration from the most unusual sources.

Probably the biggest thank you should go to my parents for bringing me into the world and giving me the opportunity to experience life. Being a parent is a tough job, and we continuously worry about whether we're doing it right. Well, let me tell you both right now, you did an amazing job! All a parent really wants for their children is for them to be happy and I'd safely say you've accomplished that.

Adam, you are the best big brother anybody could ever wish for and the laughs we shared growing up will live on in my memory until the day I die. Even though we see less of each other nowadays, that special bond remains, just like when we were kids. You still are, and always will be one of my biggest heroes.

Thanks to Ryan, Joshua and Lucy for putting a smile on my face every day. Each moment with you is precious, and watching your unique personalities develop is an absolute pleasure. I love you all so much and remember; all I want is for each of you to be happy no matter how. So, go out there and make it happen every day.

To my in-laws Mark and Carole; thanks for everything you do, but most of all, thank you for producing the centre of my world — your beautiful daughter.

Countless times we've been told we are the perfect couple, and I honestly agree. But I have chuckled at the number of times this book has caused an argument between us, which is ironic I know — but it's the truth.

If I told you my life was like living inside a bubble of pure happiness, where I smiled constantly and never complained, I'd be lying. But this is the problem — we're all after perfection, just like our friends' social media profiles.

This type of perfection doesn't exist, but I can honestly say that my life really is perfect because I appreciate that it's meant to be imperfect.

Life is full of ups and downs like a roller coaster ride, but I love it.

And that's mostly to do with the life I share with Claire. I wouldn't change a second of our past for anything.

I wasn't using my book writing to get out of the housework, I just wanted to give everyone the opportunity to be as happy as us.

Love you forever xxxx

ABOUT THE AUTHOR

Dominic King is a professional judo and mixed martial arts coach, running his own business 'Dominic King Judo & MMA Academy' in the East of England.

As a judo competitor, he won British and International titles, and trained all over the world.

In 2015, Dominic wrote a book called 'Judo Armbars For Mixed Martial Arts' and he really enjoyed the experience.

This encouraged him to write a new book, but this time on a very different subject – happiness.

Dominic had been extremely happy all his life, but also had a good understanding of psychology due to his fight career. Despite this, Dominic questioned his own knowledge and expertise, so began studying the psychology of success and happiness on a daily basis, and still does to this day.

It didn't take long to recognise why he was so happy and why many people struggled – the patterns were obvious and he shares his discoveries and experience in *World Class Happiness*.

He is also happily married with 3 beautiful children

Printed in Great Britain
by Amazon